Table Of Contents

~ *Welcome & What You'll Learn*

Section 1: Introduction to Airtable

Chapter 1: Understanding the No-Code Movement — *Pg no. 5*
Chapter 2: What Is Airtable? — *Pg no. 8*
Chapter 3: Key Airtable Terminology — *Pg no. 11*
Chapter 4: Setting Up Your Account and Workspace — *Pg no. 14*

Section 2: Laying the Foundation

Chapter 5: Creating Your First Base — *Pg no. 17*
Chapter 6: Working with Tables and Fields — *Pg no. 20*
Chapter 7: Customizing Field Types — *Pg no. 23*
Chapter 8: Organizing and Sorting Records — *Pg no. 27*

Section 3: Views and Collaboration

Chapter 9: Exploring Different View Types — *Pg no. 31*
Chapter 10: Filtering, Grouping, and Color-Coding — *Pg no. 36*
Chapter 11: Sharing Bases and Permissions — *Pg no. 39*
Chapter 12: Revision History and Collaboration Tips — *Pg no. 42*

Section 4: Data Linking and Advanced Fields

Chapter 13: Linked Records and Rollups — *Pg no. 45*
Chapter 14: Lookups and Formula Fields — *Pg no. 49*
Chapter 15: Creating Master-Detail Relationships — *Pg no. 53*
Chapter 16: Best Practices for Data Relationships — *Pg no. 57*

Section 5: Using Forms for Data Collection

Chapter 17: Designing Forms in Airtable — *Pg no. 61*
Chapter 18: Managing Form Responses — *Pg no. 65*
Chapter 19: Embedding Forms on Websites — *Pg no. 69*
Chapter 20: Streamlining Form-Based Workflows — *Pg no. 73*

Section 6: Automations and Integrations

Chapter 21: Introduction to Airtable Automations — *Pg no. 77*
Chapter 22: Setting Up Automated Triggers — *Pg no. 81*
Chapter 23: Integrating with Third-Party Services — *Pg no. 84*
Chapter 24: Optimizing Automated Workflows — *Pg no. 88*

Section 7: Building Interfaces and Web Apps

Chapter 25: Introduction to Interfaces — *Pg no. 92*
Chapter 26: Creating a Simple Interface for Your Base — *Pg no. 96*
Chapter 27: Publishing Your Interface as a Web App — *Pg no. 99*
Chapter 28: Styling and Customization Options — *Pg no. 103*

Section 8: Beyond the Basics

Chapter 29: Scripting with Airtable — *Pg no. 106*
Chapter 30: Using Blocks for Extended Functionality — *Pg no. 110*
Chapter 31: Performance Considerations — *Pg no. 114*
Chapter 32: Troubleshooting Common Issues — *Pg no. 118*

Section 9: Practical Use Cases

Chapter 33: Project Management and Task Tracking — *Pg no. 122*
Chapter 34: CRM and Sales Pipelines — *Pg no. 126*
Chapter 35: Content Calendar and Editorial Planning — *Pg no. 130*
Chapter 36: Inventory Management and Asset Tracking — *Pg no. 134*

Section 10: Best Practices and Maintenance

Chapter 37: Data Backup and Recovery Strategies — *Pg no. 138*
Chapter 38: Security and Compliance in Airtable — *Pg no. 142*
Chapter 39: Scaling Up: Handling Larger Teams and Bases — *Pg no. 146*
Chapter 40: Documentation and Team Training — *Pg no. 150*
Chapter 41: Common Pitfalls to Avoid — *Pg no. 153*

Appendices

- Appendix A: Glossary of Airtable Terms
- Appendix B: Keyboard Shortcuts and Productivity Tips
- Appendix C: Additional Resources and Recommended Tools

~ Conclusion

Welcome & What You'll Learn

Welcome to "Airtable Made Easy: From Data Management to Powerful Web Apps"

Congratulations on taking the first step toward mastering Airtable! Whether you're new to Airtable or have dabbled in it before, this book will serve as your ultimate guide to unlocking its full potential. Airtable is more than just a database tool—it's a versatile platform that allows you to manage data, automate workflows, and even build fully functional web applications, all without writing a single line of code.

This book is designed to provide a seamless learning experience, guiding you step by step from the basics to advanced topics. By the time you finish, you'll have the skills and confidence to use Airtable for everything from organizing personal projects to building professional-grade tools for your business.

Why Airtable?

Airtable stands out because it combines the simplicity of a spreadsheet with the power of a database. Its user-friendly interface makes it accessible to beginners, while its robust features make it indispensable for advanced users. As the no-code movement grows, Airtable has become a cornerstone tool for individuals and teams seeking to innovate without relying on traditional coding.

Whether you're managing a project, tracking sales leads, or automating workflows, Airtable's adaptability makes it an ideal choice for a wide variety of use cases. With its integration capabilities and customization options, you can tailor it to meet your unique needs.

Who Is This Book For?

This book is for anyone who wants to:

- **Get Started with Airtable**: Beginners will learn the fundamentals of Airtable, from setting up an account to creating their first database.
- **Master Advanced Features**: Intermediate users will deepen their understanding of linked records, automations, and custom interfaces.
- **Streamline Workflows**: Teams and organizations will learn how to use Airtable to enhance collaboration, manage data efficiently, and automate repetitive tasks.
- **Build No-Code Applications**: Entrepreneurs and developers will explore how to leverage Airtable to create functional web apps without writing code.

What You'll Learn

Here's a sneak peek at what you can expect to gain from this book:

1. Fundamentals of Airtable

- The basics of the no-code movement and why Airtable is a game-changer.
- Setting up your account, creating bases, and understanding key terminology.

2. Organizing and Managing Data

- How to create and customize tables, fields, and records.
- Sorting, filtering, and organizing your data for maximum efficiency.

3. Collaboration and Sharing

- Learn how to share your Airtable bases with others and set appropriate permissions.

- Tips for managing revision history and fostering seamless team collaboration.

4. Advanced Features and Automation

- Explore linked records, rollups, and formula fields for complex data relationships.
- Master Airtable automations to streamline tasks and improve productivity.

5. Building Custom Interfaces and Web Apps

- Step-by-step guidance on creating interfaces and turning them into web apps.
- Customization tips to make your applications user-friendly and visually appealing.

6. Practical Use Cases

- Real-world applications for project management, CRM, content calendars, and more.
- Industry-specific examples to inspire your creativity and problem-solving skills.

7. Best Practices and Troubleshooting

- Strategies for data backup, security, and scaling your Airtable projects.
- Common pitfalls to avoid and how to troubleshoot effectively.

How to Use This Book

This book is divided into sections that gradually build on each other. If you're new to Airtable, it's recommended that you start at the beginning and work your way through. If you're already familiar with the basics, feel free to jump to the sections that interest you the most.

Each chapter includes actionable steps, practical tips, and examples to help you apply what you've learned. By following along, you'll be able to see immediate results and build confidence in your skills.

Let's Get Started

Airtable has the potential to transform how you manage data and workflows. By the end of this book, you'll not only understand the ins and outs of Airtable but also be equipped to use it as a powerful tool for innovation and efficiency.

Let's dive in and begin your Airtable journey!

Section 1:
Introduction to Airtable

Understanding the No-Code Movement

The no-code movement is a revolutionary approach to software development that empowers individuals and businesses to create applications and solutions without the need for traditional coding. By leveraging intuitive tools and user-friendly interfaces, no-code platforms democratize technology, enabling anyone—regardless of technical expertise—to build functional software.

At its core, the no-code movement breaks down the barriers between ideas and execution. You no longer need to rely solely on developers or invest heavily in complex programming languages to bring your vision to life. Instead, you can use drag-and-drop functionality, pre-built templates, and visual workflows to design systems tailored to your needs.

Why Is the No-Code Movement Growing?

The rapid growth of the no-code movement is driven by several factors:

1. Accessibility

No-code platforms eliminate the steep learning curve associated with traditional programming. This allows non-technical users—such as entrepreneurs, small business owners, and project managers—to create solutions independently.

2. Speed

With no-code tools, you can prototype, build, and deploy applications in a fraction of the time it takes to code them from scratch. This agility is particularly valuable in fast-paced industries or when responding to changing business needs.

3. Cost-Effectiveness

Hiring developers and maintaining custom-coded software can be expensive. No-code platforms reduce these costs by enabling you to build and manage applications internally, often at a fraction of the cost.

4. Customization

While off-the-shelf software may not fit every need, no-code platforms provide the flexibility to create highly customized solutions that align with your specific requirements.

5. Empowering Innovation

The no-code movement fosters innovation by giving individuals and teams the tools to experiment, iterate, and bring their ideas to life without relying on technical bottlenecks.

Key Characteristics of No-Code Platforms

No-code platforms like Airtable share common features that make them accessible and powerful:

- **Visual Interfaces**: Users interact with intuitive, graphical interfaces instead of writing code.
- **Drag-and-Drop Functionality**: Elements can be easily added, arranged, and customized without technical complexity.
- **Pre-Built Templates**: Many no-code platforms offer ready-to-use templates for common use cases, such as project management or customer relationship management (CRM).
- **Integrations**: Seamless connectivity with other tools and services through APIs and pre-built integrations.
- **Automation**: Built-in tools to automate repetitive tasks and streamline workflows.

The Role of Airtable in the No-Code Movement

Airtable is one of the leading platforms driving the no-code revolution. Its combination of database functionality and user-friendly design makes it a versatile tool for individuals and businesses alike.

With Airtable, you can:

- Create and organize data in a way that's as easy as using a spreadsheet.
- Build workflows, track projects, and manage teams with custom bases.
- Automate tasks and connect with other apps, enhancing productivity and efficiency.
- Design forms, interfaces, and even web apps—all without writing a single line of code.

The Benefits of Embracing No-Code Solutions

Adopting no-code tools like Airtable can transform how you approach problem-solving and innovation. Here's how:

1. Empowering Teams

No-code tools encourage collaboration by enabling non-technical team members to actively contribute to building and managing solutions.

2. Boosting Productivity

By automating repetitive tasks and centralizing data, no-code platforms free up time for higher-value work.

3. Encouraging Experimentation

The low-risk nature of no-code tools allows you to experiment with new ideas, test workflows, and iterate quickly.

4. Increasing Agility

In today's fast-paced world, the ability to adapt to changing circumstances is critical. No-code platforms provide the flexibility to adjust and scale your solutions as needed.

Common Myths About No-Code

Despite its advantages, some misconceptions about no-code solutions persist. Let's address a few:

- **"No-code is only for simple projects."** While no-code platforms excel at straightforward tasks, they're also powerful enough to handle complex workflows and advanced automation.
- **"No-code tools are not secure."** Leading platforms like Airtable prioritize data security, offering enterprise-grade compliance and robust permissions settings.
- **"Developers don't use no-code tools."** On the contrary, developers often use no-code tools to speed up prototyping, streamline workflows, or complement traditional coding efforts.

How This Chapter Sets the Stage

Understanding the no-code movement is essential to appreciating the power and versatility of Airtable. As you move through this book, you'll see how Airtable embodies the principles of no-code: simplicity, flexibility, and accessibility.

Whether you're a business professional looking to streamline operations or an entrepreneur ready to build your next big idea, the no-code movement—and Airtable in particular—offers the tools to make it happen.

Let's dive deeper into Airtable and see how it can transform your workflows, data management, and creative projects!

What Is Airtable?

Airtable is a powerful no-code platform that combines the simplicity of a spreadsheet with the robustness of a database. It's designed to help individuals, teams, and businesses organize data, collaborate seamlessly, and build custom workflows. Whether you're managing personal projects or complex business processes, Airtable adapts to your needs with its flexibility and ease of use.

The Core of Airtable

At its heart, Airtable is a **relational database**, meaning it allows you to store, manage, and connect data across multiple tables. Unlike traditional databases, Airtable provides a user-friendly interface that eliminates the technical complexity associated with database management. It's intuitive enough for beginners yet powerful enough for advanced users.

Airtable is often described as "spreadsheets on steroids," but it's much more than that. While spreadsheets are great for simple data organization, Airtable offers features like linked records, customizable field types, and automation capabilities that make it a game-changer for data management.

Why Use Airtable?

Airtable stands out because it bridges the gap between spreadsheets and databases while adding modern functionality. Here's why it's worth using:

1. Ease of Use

Airtable's interface is clean, visually appealing, and easy to navigate. Even if you're new to data management, you can start building bases (Airtable's version of a database) in no time.

2. Versatility

From project management and inventory tracking to CRM systems and editorial planning, Airtable can be tailored to fit virtually any use case.

3. Collaboration

Airtable excels as a collaborative tool, allowing multiple users to work on the same base in real time. You can set permissions, leave comments, and track changes effortlessly.

4. Automation and Integration

Airtable's automation features and integration options with tools like Zapier, Slack, and Google Workspace enable you to streamline workflows and save time.

5. No-Code Development

Airtable empowers users to build custom apps and interfaces without requiring any programming knowledge. This makes it an ideal tool for entrepreneurs, small business owners, and teams seeking agility.

Key Features of Airtable

1. Bases

A **base** is the foundation of Airtable, similar to a file in a spreadsheet application. Each base consists of multiple tables, where you can store and organize your data.

2. Tables and Fields

A base is made up of **tables**, which function like individual spreadsheets. Each table contains **fields** (columns) and **records** (rows). Fields can be customized to include various data types, such as text, numbers, dates, attachments, and more.

3. Views

Airtable provides **views** to help you display and interact with your data in different ways. Common view types include grid view (spreadsheet-style), calendar view, gallery view, and kanban view.

4. Linked Records

One of Airtable's standout features is the ability to create **linked records** between tables. This allows you to establish relationships between data, similar to how relational databases work.

5. Automations

Airtable lets you automate repetitive tasks with triggers and actions. For example, you can set up an automation to send an email when a record is updated or to create tasks in a project management tool when new data is added.

6. Forms

Airtable includes built-in form functionality, making it easy to collect data from external users and have it automatically populate your tables.

7. Integration and APIs

Airtable integrates with hundreds of tools, such as Slack, Zapier, Google Drive, and Microsoft Teams. Additionally, its robust API makes it a developer-friendly platform for custom integrations.

Airtable's Role in the No-Code Ecosystem

Airtable plays a crucial role in the growing no-code movement by enabling users to create applications and workflows without writing code. Its flexibility and scalability make it an ideal tool for:

- **Small Businesses**: Manage operations, track sales, and handle inventory.
- **Enterprises**: Collaborate across teams, manage complex projects, and create custom tools.
- **Individuals**: Organize personal projects, budgets, and creative pursuits.

Real-World Examples of Airtable in Action

Here are some practical examples of how Airtable is used across different industries:

- **Marketing Teams**: Plan campaigns, manage content calendars, and track performance metrics.
- **Product Teams**: Manage feature backlogs, gather customer feedback, and track development progress.
- **Event Planners**: Organize events, track RSVPs, and manage vendor relationships.

- **Nonprofits**: Track donations, manage volunteers, and coordinate outreach programs.

The Airtable Advantage

Airtable's adaptability is its greatest strength. Whether you're managing a simple task list or building a complex CRM system, Airtable can scale to meet your needs. Its intuitive interface ensures that anyone can get started quickly, while its advanced features make it a powerful tool for seasoned users.

Key Airtable Terminology

Before diving into the practical applications of Airtable, it's crucial to familiarize yourself with its core terminology. Understanding these terms will help you navigate Airtable effectively and make the most of its features. Think of this as your foundation for building and managing powerful Airtable workflows.

The Essential Terms

1. Base

A **base** is Airtable's version of a database. It's the starting point for organizing your data and can contain multiple tables. Each base is designed for a specific project or purpose, such as tracking tasks, managing inventory, or planning events.

- Example: A marketing team might create a base for managing social media campaigns, with tables for scheduling posts, tracking performance metrics, and managing content creators.

2. Table

A **table** is like a spreadsheet within a base. It organizes your data into rows (records) and columns (fields). You can have multiple tables in a single base, and they can be linked together for advanced functionality.

- Example: In a project management base, you could have one table for tasks, another for team members, and another for project milestones.

3. Field

A **field** is a column in a table that stores a specific type of information, such as text, numbers, dates, attachments, or formulas. Fields are highly customizable, allowing you to define the type of data each column will accept.

- Common field types:
  - Single line text
  - Long text
  - Date
  - Checkbox
  - Dropdowns (Single Select or Multiple Select)
  - Attachments

4. Record

A **record** is a row in a table that represents an individual item or entry. Each record can contain multiple pieces of information stored in the fields.

- Example: In an inventory table, each record could represent a unique product, with fields for the product name, SKU, quantity, and price.

5. View

A **view** is a customizable way to display and interact with your table's data. Airtable offers multiple view types to help you focus on specific aspects of your data.

- Common view types:
  - **Grid View**: A spreadsheet-like layout.
  - **Calendar View**: Displays records based on date fields.

- ○ **Gallery View**: Shows records as cards with images or key details.
- ○ **Kanban View**: Organizes records into stacks, ideal for workflows.

6. Linked Record

A **linked record** connects data between two tables. This is one of Airtable's most powerful features, allowing you to create relationships between tables.

- Example: In a CRM base, you could link a "Clients" table to a "Projects" table to track which clients are associated with which projects.

7. Rollup Field

A **rollup field** aggregates data from linked records, such as summing up values or finding the average.

- Example: In an invoicing table, a rollup field could calculate the total amount billed to a client by summing up all associated invoice records.

8. Lookup Field

A **lookup field** pulls specific information from a linked record.

- Example: In a project management base, you could use a lookup field to display the email addresses of team members assigned to a task.

9. Formula Field

A **formula field** performs calculations or manipulations based on other fields in the table. Airtable's formula editor supports a wide range of functions, from simple arithmetic to advanced conditional logic.

- Example: Create a formula field to calculate the total cost of a product by multiplying its quantity by its unit price.

10. Automation

Automations are workflows that you can set up to perform tasks automatically based on triggers. They save time by reducing the need for manual intervention.

- Example: Create an automation to send a notification email whenever a new record is added to a table.

11. Form

A **form** is a user-friendly interface for collecting data. When someone fills out the form, their responses populate the associated table in Airtable.

- Example: Use a form to collect feedback from customers, with the responses automatically added to your feedback table.

12. Workspace

A **workspace** is the container for all your bases. Workspaces are typically organized by teams or departments within an organization.

- Example: A company could have separate workspaces for marketing, sales, and operations, each containing bases relevant to those teams.

13. Revision History

Airtable keeps track of changes made to records, allowing you to view the **revision history** and restore previous versions if needed.

- Example: If a teammate accidentally deletes data, you can use revision history to recover it.

14. Sync

The **sync** feature allows you to connect tables across different bases or workspaces. Updates in one table are automatically reflected in the synced table.

- Example: Sync a sales table from a CRM base with a project management base to keep both teams aligned.

15. Permissions

Permissions control who can access and edit your Airtable bases and tables. You can set different levels of access for collaborators, such as editor, commenter, or viewer.

- Example: Grant full editing access to team members while restricting clients to view-only access.

Why Understanding Airtable Terminology Matters

A clear understanding of Airtable's terminology is essential for building effective workflows and avoiding confusion. As you progress through this book, these terms will come up repeatedly, and knowing them will help you follow along seamlessly.

Putting It into Practice

Now that you're familiar with Airtable's key terminology, you're ready to start exploring its features in greater detail. The next chapter will guide you through setting up your account and workspace, laying the foundation for your Airtable journey.

Let's get started!

Setting Up Your Account and Workspace

Before diving into Airtable's powerful features, the first step is to create your account and set up your workspace. This chapter will guide you through the process, ensuring you're ready to build and manage your data effectively. By the end, you'll have a functional Airtable account and an organized workspace tailored to your needs.

Creating Your Airtable Account

Setting up an Airtable account is quick and straightforward. Follow these steps to get started:

1. Visit Airtable's Website

Go to www.airtable.com and click on the "Sign Up" button in the top-right corner.

2. Choose a Signup Method

Airtable offers multiple ways to sign up:

- **Email Address**: Enter your email, create a password, and verify your email address.
- **Google Account**: Use your Google credentials for faster setup.
- **Apple ID**: Sign up using your Apple account.

3. Complete Your Profile

After signing up, you'll be prompted to provide some basic details, such as your name and intended use for Airtable.

4. Confirm Your Email

Check your email inbox for a verification message from Airtable. Click on the link provided to verify your account.

Congratulations! You now have an Airtable account and can start exploring the platform.

Navigating the Airtable Dashboard

Once you log in, you'll be taken to the **Airtable Dashboard**. This is your central hub for accessing all your bases and workspaces. Let's break it down:

1. Workspaces

Workspaces are the organizational units within Airtable. They group related bases together, making it easier to manage projects, teams, or departments.

- Example: You can create separate workspaces for personal projects, marketing campaigns, or client accounts.

2. Bases

Bases are listed within each workspace. Each base represents a specific database or project. You'll use bases to store and manage your data.

3. Sidebar Navigation

The left-hand sidebar displays your workspaces and their associated bases. You can switch between workspaces or create new ones here.

4. Account Menu

In the top-right corner, you'll find the account menu, where you can update your profile, adjust settings, and manage your subscription.

Setting Up Your Workspace

Airtable workspaces are highly customizable, allowing you to structure them to fit your needs. Follow these steps to set up your first workspace:

1. Create a New Workspace

- Click on the "+ Add a workspace" button in the sidebar.
- Name your workspace based on its purpose, such as "Marketing Team" or "Personal Projects."

2. Adjust Workspace Settings

You can access workspace settings by clicking the dropdown arrow next to the workspace name. Here, you can:

- **Invite Collaborators**: Add team members and assign permissions (editor, commenter, or viewer).
- **Upgrade Plans**: If needed, you can upgrade to a premium plan for additional features like advanced permissions or more storage.
- **Rename the Workspace**: Update the name if necessary.

3. Add Bases to the Workspace

Once your workspace is created, you can start adding bases to organize your data. You'll learn how to create bases in the next chapter.

Collaborating Within a Workspace

One of Airtable's strengths is its collaboration features. Here's how you can set up a collaborative workspace:

1. Invite Team Members

- Click the "Share" button in the top-right corner of the workspace or base.
- Enter the email addresses of your collaborators.
- Assign appropriate permissions:
    - **Editor**: Can make changes to the data and structure.
    - **Commenter**: Can add comments but not edit data.
    - **Viewer**: Can only view the data.

2. Set Permissions

Airtable allows you to set granular permissions at the workspace or base level. This ensures that sensitive data remains secure while allowing collaboration where needed.

3. Communicate and Collaborate

Collaborators can leave comments on records, tag teammates using "@mentions," and see changes in real time.

Customizing Your Workspace

To make your workspace more functional, consider these customization tips:

1. Use Color-Coding

Airtable allows you to color-code bases to make them visually distinct. Use colors to group similar projects or prioritize important tasks.

2. Organize Bases by Purpose

Arrange your bases in a logical order within the workspace. For example, group marketing-related bases together or list project phases sequentially.

3. Add Base Descriptions

You can add a short description to each base to clarify its purpose. This is especially helpful in shared workspaces.

Best Practices for Workspace Organization

To ensure your workspace remains efficient and organized, follow these best practices:

- **Keep Workspaces Focused**: Create separate workspaces for distinct teams or purposes to avoid clutter.
- **Regularly Review Permissions**: Periodically check and update collaborator permissions to maintain security.
- **Archive Old Bases**: For completed projects, archive or move bases to a dedicated "Archive" workspace to keep your active workspaces tidy.

Conclusion

Setting up your Airtable account and workspace is the first step toward leveraging the platform's full potential. With a well-structured workspace, you'll have a solid foundation for managing data, collaborating with others, and building powerful workflows.

Section 2:
Laying the Foundation

Creating Your First Base

A base is the foundational building block in Airtable. It functions as a single database where you can store, organize, and manage data related to a specific project or purpose. In this chapter, you'll learn how to create your first base, understand its structure, and set it up to suit your needs.

Whether you're starting from scratch or using a template, creating a base is simple and intuitive. By the end of this chapter, you'll have a fully functional base ready to help you streamline your workflows.

Step 1: Starting a New Base

Airtable offers two ways to create a new base: from scratch or by using a template. Let's explore both options.

1. Creating a Base from Scratch

- Navigate to your workspace in the Airtable dashboard.
- Click the "+ Add a base" button at the bottom of the workspace.
- Select **"Start from scratch"**.
- Name your base and choose a color and icon to represent it visually. This is especially useful for identifying your bases at a glance.

2. Using a Template

Airtable provides a library of pre-built templates designed for common use cases such as project management, CRM, or content planning.

- Click the "+ Add a base" button.
- Select **"Use a template"** and browse the categories to find a template that matches your needs.
- Customize the template by renaming tables, fields, and views to suit your workflow.

Pro Tip: If you're new to Airtable, starting with a template can help you learn by example. You can always modify it as you grow more comfortable with the platform.

Step 2: Understanding the Structure of a Base

A base is composed of the following elements:

1. Tables

Each base contains one or more tables, which function like individual spreadsheets. Tables are where you'll organize your data into rows and columns.

2. Fields

Fields are the columns in your tables, defining the type of information each record will store (e.g., text, numbers, dates).

3. Records

Records are the rows in your tables, representing individual entries or items.

4. Views

Views allow you to display and interact with your data in different formats, such as grids, calendars, galleries, or kanban boards.

Step 3: Setting Up Your Base

After creating your base, it's time to set it up for your specific project or workflow. Follow these steps:

1. Add Tables

Start by naming your first table based on the type of data it will store. For example, if you're managing a project, you might create tables for "Tasks," "Team Members," and "Milestones."

- To add a new table, click the "+" tab at the bottom of the base.
- Rename the table by double-clicking its name.

2. Customize Fields

Each table comes with default fields, but you can customize them to match your needs.

- Rename fields by double-clicking their headers.
- Choose a field type (e.g., single-line text, checkbox, dropdown) that suits the data you want to store.

3. Add Records

Enter data directly into the table by clicking on a cell and typing. Each row represents a record, such as a task, a product, or a contact.

4. Save and Organize Data

Airtable saves changes automatically, so there's no need to manually save your work. Use the drag-and-drop functionality to reorder fields and records as needed.

Step 4: Enhancing Your Base

Once your base is set up, you can enhance it with additional features to improve functionality and organization.

1. Create Linked Tables

Linking tables allows you to create relationships between data, such as associating tasks with team members.

- Add a "Linked Record" field to a table and link it to another table in the same base.

2. Use Color Coding

Color-code records based on specific criteria to make your data more visually intuitive. For example, use colors to highlight high-priority tasks or overdue deadlines.

3. Add Views

Create different views to display your data in ways that best suit your workflow. For example:

- **Grid View** for a spreadsheet-like layout.
- **Calendar View** for scheduling tasks or events.
- **Kanban View** for tracking project progress visually.

4. Add Collaborators

Invite team members to collaborate on your base. Use the "Share" button to add collaborators and set permissions (e.g., editor, commenter, viewer).

Step 5: Save and Reuse Your Base

Once your base is fully set up, you can save it as a template for future use.

- Click the dropdown arrow next to the base name.
- Select **"Duplicate base"** to create a copy for a new project.

Common Mistakes to Avoid

- **Overcomplicating the Structure**: Start simple and add complexity as needed. Avoid creating too many tables or fields at the beginning.
- **Skipping Linked Tables**: Use linked tables to maintain data relationships instead of duplicating information across tables.
- **Ignoring Permissions**: Set appropriate permissions for collaborators to avoid accidental changes or data loss.

Conclusion

Creating your first base is an exciting step in your Airtable journey. With a well-structured base, you'll be able to organize your data, collaborate with others, and streamline your workflows.

Working with Tables and Fields

Tables and fields are the core components of any Airtable base. Tables help you organize data into structured groups, while fields define the type of data stored in each column. By mastering tables and fields, you can efficiently structure your information and make it easier to manage and analyze.

This chapter will guide you through the essential steps of creating and working with tables, customizing fields, and understanding how these components interact to form a solid foundation for your Airtable workflows.

Understanding Tables in Airtable

What Are Tables?

A table in Airtable is similar to a sheet in a traditional spreadsheet application. Each table contains rows (records) and columns (fields), and tables within a base can be linked together to create relational databases.

For example, in a project management base, you might have:

- A "Tasks" table to list all project tasks.
- A "Team Members" table to store information about the people involved.
- A "Milestones" table to track project goals.

How to Create a Table

- **From Scratch**:
    1. Open your base and click the "+" tab at the bottom of the screen.
    2. Select **"Add or import a table"**.
    3. Name your table to reflect its purpose.
- **From Templates**:
  Airtable provides pre-built table templates for common use cases. To use a template, select it from the template library when adding a new table.

Customizing Table Settings

- **Renaming Tables**: Double-click the table's name and type the new name.
- **Reordering Tables**: Drag and drop tables to rearrange their order within the base.
- **Deleting Tables**: Click the dropdown arrow next to the table's name and select "Delete table."

Exploring Fields in Airtable

What Are Fields?

Fields are the columns in a table, and they determine the type of data stored in each record. Airtable offers a wide variety of field types, allowing you to customize your table to suit your data needs.

Types of Fields

Here are some of the most commonly used field types:

- **Single Line Text**: For short text entries like names or titles.

- **Long Text**: For detailed descriptions or notes.
- **Number**: For numerical data, such as quantities or costs.
- **Checkbox**: For binary options, such as marking tasks as complete.
- **Date**: For dates and times.
- **Single Select**: For predefined options where only one can be selected (e.g., task status: "To Do," "In Progress," "Done").
- **Multiple Select**: For predefined options where multiple selections are allowed (e.g., skill sets: "Design," "Coding," "Marketing").
- **Attachment**: For uploading files, such as images or PDFs.
- **Link to Another Record**: For creating relationships between tables.
- **Formula**: For performing calculations or conditional logic.

How to Add and Customize Fields

- To add a field:
    1. Click the "+" icon at the top-right corner of the table.
    2. Select the field type from the dropdown menu.
    3. Name the field and configure any additional settings (e.g., default values, formatting).
- To customize a field:
    1. Click the dropdown arrow in the field's header.
    2. Select **"Customize field type"** to change the type or settings.

Tips for Organizing Fields

- Use clear and descriptive names for each field.
- Group related fields together for easier navigation.
- Delete unused fields to reduce clutter.

Adding and Managing Records

Records are the rows in your table, representing individual entries. For example, in a "Tasks" table, each record could represent a single task.

How to Add Records

- **Manually**: Click the "+" button at the bottom of the table and fill in the fields for the new record.
- **Importing Data**: Use the "Import" option to bring in data from spreadsheets, CSV files, or external sources.
- **Forms**: Create a form view to collect data from external users, which automatically populates the table with new records.

Editing and Deleting Records

- To edit a record, click on a cell and type the new value.
- To delete a record, right-click the row number and select **"Delete record."**

Best Practices for Tables and Fields

1. Keep Tables Focused

Each table should represent a single entity or concept. For example, keep "Tasks" and "Team Members" in separate tables, and use linked records to connect them.

2. Choose the Right Field Types

Select field types that match your data to ensure accuracy and consistency. For instance, use a date field for deadlines instead of a text field.

3. Use Default Values

Set default values for fields like "Status" or "Priority" to save time when adding new records.

4. Avoid Duplicate Data

Leverage linked records to avoid duplicating information across tables. For example, instead of entering a team member's name in multiple places, link their record from the "Team Members" table.

5. Regularly Review and Clean Up Data

Periodically review your tables and fields to ensure they remain organized and relevant. Archive or delete old records and fields as necessary.

Common Challenges and Solutions

Challenge 1: Too Many Fields

Having too many fields can make your table cluttered and hard to navigate.

- **Solution**: Group related data into separate tables and use linked records.

Challenge 2: Choosing the Wrong Field Type

Using the wrong field type can lead to inconsistent data entry.

- **Solution**: Choose field types based on the type of data you plan to store.

Challenge 3: Duplicate Records

Duplicate records can make your data messy and unreliable.

- **Solution**: Regularly audit your tables for duplicates and use linked records to maintain data relationships.

Conclusion

Tables and fields form the backbone of any Airtable base. By mastering these components, you can create organized, efficient, and flexible systems to manage your data. With the right structure in place, you'll be well-equipped to streamline workflows and unlock Airtable's full potential.

Customizing Field Types

In Airtable, fields are the backbone of your tables, defining the type of data that each column will store. By customizing field types, you can structure your data more effectively and ensure consistency across your base. This chapter explores the various field types available in Airtable, how to customize them to fit your needs, and tips for optimizing your workflow.

Customizing field types is essential for creating dynamic, flexible, and powerful bases that cater to your unique requirements.

Why Customizing Field Types Matters

Using the right field types helps:

- Ensure accurate and consistent data entry.
- Enhance the usability and clarity of your tables.
- Unlock advanced features, such as calculations, automation, and linked relationships.

Overview of Field Types

Airtable offers a wide range of field types to accommodate different types of data. Below is an overview of the most commonly used field types:

1. Single Line Text

- Best for: Short text entries, such as names or titles.
- Example: "Task Name" or "Customer Name."

2. Long Text

- Best for: Detailed descriptions or notes.
- Example: "Task Details" or "Product Descriptions."

3. Number

- Best for: Storing numerical data, such as quantities or monetary values.
- Example: "Inventory Count" or "Product Price."

4. Checkbox

- Best for: Tracking binary options (yes/no or complete/incomplete).
- Example: "Task Completed" checkbox to track progress.

5. Date

- Best for: Storing dates and times.
- Example: "Due Date" or "Event Date."

6. Single Select

- Best for: Choosing one option from a predefined list.
- Example: "Task Status" with options like "To Do," "In Progress," and "Done."

7. Multiple Select

- Best for: Selecting multiple options from a predefined list.
- Example: "Skills" with options like "Design," "Development," and "Marketing."

8. Attachment

- Best for: Uploading files, images, or documents.
- Example: "Project Files" or "Product Images."

9. Link to Another Record

- Best for: Creating relationships between tables.
- Example: Linking "Tasks" to "Team Members."

10. Formula

- Best for: Performing calculations or creating conditional logic.
- Example: Calculating total cost using "Quantity × Unit Price."

11. Rollup

- Best for: Aggregating data from linked tables.
- Example: Summing up "Total Hours Worked" for a project.

12. Lookup

- Best for: Displaying data from linked records.
- Example: Showing a client's email address in a project table.

13. Currency

- Best for: Financial data.
- Example: "Budget" or "Sales Revenue."

14. Rating

- Best for: Ranking or scoring items.
- Example: "Customer Satisfaction Rating."

15. URL

- Best for: Storing web links.
- Example: "Website" or "Documentation Link."

16. Email and Phone Number

- Best for: Contact details.
- Example: "Customer Email" or "Support Hotline."

How to Customize Field Types

Step 1: Adding a New Field

- Click the "+" icon at the top-right corner of the table to add a new field.
- Name the field and select a field type from the dropdown menu.

Step 2: Changing an Existing Field Type

- Click the dropdown arrow in the field's header.
- Select **"Customize field type."**
- Choose a new field type and configure any additional settings.

Step 3: Configuring Field Options

Many field types come with additional customization options:

- **Single Select and Multiple Select**: Add or remove options, assign colors for better visibility, and reorder choices.
- **Date Fields**: Enable time tracking or set a specific format (e.g., MM/DD/YYYY).
- **Number Fields**: Configure formatting options, such as decimal places or currency symbols.
- **Checkboxes**: Add default states for quicker data entry.

Tips for Effective Field Customization

1. Use Descriptive Field Names

Choose clear and specific names for your fields so collaborators can easily understand their purpose.

2. Group Related Fields

Arrange fields logically to make your table more intuitive. For example, group all contact-related fields (e.g., name, phone, email) together.

3. Limit Options for Select Fields

For fields like Single Select or Multiple Select, limit options to maintain consistency. Avoid allowing free-text input for categorical data.

4. Use Default Values

Set default values for fields like "Status" or "Priority" to save time during data entry.

5. Leverage Linked Fields

Use "Link to Another Record" fields to connect related data instead of duplicating information across tables.

6. Test Your Setup

Before finalizing your table structure, test your fields by entering sample data to ensure they work as intended.

Advanced Field Customization

1. Formulas for Calculations

- Combine fields to create new insights.
- Example: Use a formula to calculate total cost by multiplying "Quantity" by "Unit Price."

2. Conditional Logic

- Use formulas to display values based on conditions.
- Example: Create a "Priority" field that shows "High" if the deadline is within 3 days.

3. Rollups and Lookups

- Aggregate data from linked tables using Rollups.
- Example: Calculate the total hours worked on a project by summing up hours logged in a linked "Tasks" table.

Common Mistakes to Avoid

Mistake 1: Using Text Fields for Dates or Numbers

Text fields don't allow for sorting, filtering, or calculations. Use Date or Number fields instead.

Mistake 2: Overcomplicating Field Types

Too many fields or overly complex setups can make your table difficult to use. Start simple and expand as needed.

Mistake 3: Ignoring Field Options

Failing to configure field options (e.g., date formats, select options) can lead to inconsistent data entry.

Conclusion

Customizing field types is a crucial step in building effective Airtable bases. By choosing the right field types and configuring them to suit your needs, you'll create tables that are not only functional but also intuitive and easy to use.

Organizing and Sorting Records

Once your tables and fields are set up in Airtable, the next step is to efficiently organize and sort your records. Properly managing your records ensures that your data is easy to navigate, accessible, and useful for making informed decisions. Whether you're tracking tasks, managing projects, or analyzing trends, learning how to organize and sort records is a fundamental skill.

This chapter will guide you through the best practices for organizing your records, using Airtable's sorting features, and maintaining a clean and structured database.

Understanding Records

What Are Records?

Records in Airtable are the rows in your table, representing individual entries or data points. For example:

- In a "Tasks" table, each record could represent a single task.
- In a "Clients" table, each record could represent a client.

Each record consists of multiple fields, and the way you organize these records impacts how efficiently you can manage and analyze your data.

Strategies for Organizing Records

1. Use Clear and Consistent Naming Conventions

- For fields that include text, such as names or titles, establish a standard naming format to ensure clarity and consistency.
- Example: Use "Last Name, First Name" for contact records or consistent task titles like "Task: [Action Item]."

2. Group Related Data Together

- Group records based on their relevance or category to make them easier to locate. For example, group tasks by project or priority level.
- Airtable's **grouping feature** helps visually organize your data by stacking records with similar field values.

3. Leverage Linked Records

- Instead of duplicating data across tables, use linked records to connect related information. For example, link a "Tasks" table to a "Team Members" table to assign tasks to specific individuals.

4. Archive or Delete Inactive Records

- Move completed or outdated records to a separate table or archive workspace to keep your active data clutter-free.

Sorting Records

Sorting allows you to reorder records in a table based on the values in one or more fields. This feature is essential for prioritizing tasks, analyzing trends, or preparing data for presentation.

How to Sort Records

1. Open the table you want to sort.
2. Click the **"Sort"** button in the toolbar.
3. Select the field(s) you want to sort by.
   ○ Example: Sort a "Tasks" table by the "Due Date" field in ascending order.
4. Choose the sorting order:
   ○ **Ascending**: Values are arranged from smallest to largest (e.g., A-Z, 1-100).
   ○ **Descending**: Values are arranged from largest to smallest (e.g., Z-A, 100-1).
5. Apply the sort. Airtable will rearrange the records based on your criteria.

Multi-Level Sorting

You can apply multiple sorting levels to further refine the order of your records:

- Example: First, sort tasks by "Priority" (e.g., High, Medium, Low), and then by "Due Date" within each priority level.

Clearing a Sort

If you want to revert the table to its original order, click the **"Clear Sort"** button.

Using Filters for Organization

Filters allow you to display only the records that meet specific criteria, making it easier to focus on relevant data.

How to Apply a Filter

1. Click the **"Filter"** button in the toolbar.
2. Select a field and define the condition.
   ○ Example: Show only tasks where the "Status" is "In Progress."
3. Add multiple filter conditions if needed. Airtable will display only the records that match all the conditions.

Common Use Cases for Filters

- Displaying tasks assigned to a specific team member.
- Highlighting overdue tasks by filtering for records where the "Due Date" is before today.
- Showing products in inventory with quantities below a certain threshold.

Grouping Records

Grouping is a powerful way to visually organize records by stacking them based on shared field values.

How to Group Records

1. Click the **"Group"** button in the toolbar.
2. Select the field you want to group by.
   ○ Example: Group a "Tasks" table by the "Project" field.

3. Airtable will create collapsible groups for each unique value in the selected field.

Nested Grouping

You can apply multiple levels of grouping for more detailed organization:

- Example: Group tasks first by "Project" and then by "Priority."

Color-Coding Records

Using colors to highlight records adds a layer of visual organization to your table.

How to Add Color Coding

1. Click the **"Color"** button in the toolbar.
2. Define color-coding rules based on specific conditions, such as field values.
   - Example: Assign a red color to tasks marked as "High Priority" and a green color to tasks marked as "Completed."

Benefits of Color Coding

- Quickly identify important records.
- Improve readability, especially in larger tables.

Best Practices for Organizing and Sorting Records

1. Keep Tables Clean and Simple

- Avoid overloading tables with unnecessary records or fields. Archive or delete data that's no longer relevant.

2. Regularly Review Data

- Periodically audit your records to ensure accuracy and consistency. Update or merge duplicate entries as needed.

3. Use Views for Different Perspectives

- Create custom views to display data tailored to specific workflows or team needs. For example, create a view that shows only "Overdue Tasks" or "Upcoming Deadlines."

4. Combine Sorting and Filtering

- Use sorting and filtering together to focus on the most relevant records in a specific order.

5. Leverage Automations

- Set up automations to categorize records or update fields automatically based on triggers.

Common Challenges and Solutions

Challenge 1: Too Many Records

Tables with too many records can become difficult to navigate.

- **Solution**: Use filters and grouping to focus on relevant data and archive old records.

Challenge 2: Inconsistent Data Entry

Inconsistent naming conventions or field values can disrupt sorting and filtering.

- **Solution**: Use Single Select fields or default values to standardize data entry.

Challenge 3: Overlapping Criteria

When sorting or filtering by multiple fields, overlapping criteria can lead to confusion.

- **Solution**: Test your sorting and filtering logic to ensure it produces the desired results.

Conclusion

Organizing and sorting records is a critical step in building efficient workflows and managing data effectively in Airtable. By mastering sorting, grouping, filtering, and color coding, you can turn even the most complex datasets into actionable insights.

Section 3:
Views and Collaboration

Exploring Different View Types

Airtable's views are a powerful feature that allows you to display and interact with your data in various formats. Views help you focus on specific aspects of your table, customize the way your data is presented, and streamline collaboration. Each view offers a unique way to analyze and manage records, making it easier to adapt Airtable to your workflow.

In this chapter, we'll explore the different view types available in Airtable, their use cases, and tips for customizing and managing views effectively.

What Are Views in Airtable?

A **view** is a customizable lens through which you can interact with the data in a table. The underlying data remains the same across all views, but the way it is displayed and organized changes based on the view settings.

For example:

- A **grid view** might show all your tasks in a spreadsheet format.
- A **calendar view** could display the same tasks organized by their due dates.

By switching between views, you can tailor your Airtable experience to meet specific needs without altering the data itself.

Types of Views in Airtable

1. Grid View

The **grid view** is Airtable's default view and resembles a traditional spreadsheet. It's ideal for general data entry, organization, and analysis.

Key Features:

- Add, edit, and delete records.
- Sort and filter data.
- Group records by specific fields.
- Freeze columns for easier navigation.

Best For:

- Data entry and maintenance.
- Viewing all records in a table at once.
- Applying sorting, filtering, and grouping to manage data efficiently.

2. Calendar View

The **calendar view** organizes records with date fields into a calendar layout. It's perfect for tracking events, deadlines, and schedules.

Key Features:

- Displays records on specific dates based on a date field.
- Supports dragging and dropping records to adjust dates.
- Shows single or multiple records on the same day.

Best For:

- Project planning and task scheduling.
- Event and campaign management.
- Visualizing deadlines and time-sensitive tasks.

3. Kanban View

The **kanban view** organizes records into stacks based on the values of a single select or multiple select field. It's a great way to track progress or manage workflows visually.

Key Features:

- Drag and drop records between stacks to update their field values.
- Customize stack order and visibility.
- Add or edit records directly within the view.

Best For:

- Workflow management (e.g., To Do, In Progress, Done).
- Agile project management and sprint planning.
- Visualizing progress or categories.

4. Gallery View

The **gallery view** displays records as large, customizable cards, making it ideal for visual data like images or detailed descriptions.

Key Features:

- Highlight a specific field or attachment as the main focus of each card.
- Customize which fields are displayed on the cards.
- Rearrange cards by dragging and dropping.

Best For:

- Showcasing images, portfolios, or products.
- Managing content libraries or creative assets.
- Visualizing records with rich descriptions or attachments.

5. Form View

The **form view** allows you to create a form for collecting data. When someone submits the form, their responses are automatically added to your table as new records.

Key Features:

- Customize fields and layout to create user-friendly forms.

- Share the form via a link or embed it on a website.
- Control which fields are visible and required.

Best For:

- Gathering feedback or survey responses.
- Collecting customer information or lead data.
- Streamlining data entry from external users.

6. Timeline View

The **timeline view** (available on certain plans) is a project management tool that visualizes records on a horizontal timeline. It's great for managing tasks and resources over time.

Key Features:

- View records along a time axis based on date fields.
- Adjust timelines by dragging and resizing records.
- Group records by categories, such as assignees or projects.

Best For:

- Gantt chart-style project planning.
- Resource allocation and scheduling.
- Tracking overlapping tasks or events.

7. Pivot Table App

Although not technically a view, the **Pivot Table App** is an advanced feature that allows you to summarize and analyze your data in a table format.

Key Features:

- Aggregate data by grouping and summarizing fields.
- Display metrics like sums, averages, and counts.
- Create customized summaries for reporting.

Best For:

- Analyzing large datasets.
- Generating performance reports.
- Summarizing data across multiple fields.

Creating and Customizing Views

How to Create a New View

1. Open the table where you want to create a view.
2. Click the "**+**" icon next to the list of views in the left sidebar.
3. Select the type of view you want to create (e.g., Grid, Calendar, Kanban).
4. Name your view and customize its settings.

Customizing View Settings

Each view type offers customization options:

- **Fields**: Choose which fields to display in the view.
- **Filters**: Apply filters to show only relevant records.
- **Sorting**: Define how records should be ordered.
- **Grouping**: Group records by specific field values for better organization.

Sharing Views

- Share a view with collaborators by clicking the **"Share"** button.
- Use the **"Share publicly"** option to generate a link for external users.

Best Practices for Using Views

1. Create Dedicated Views for Specific Tasks

- Use a grid view for data entry.
- Use a calendar view for scheduling.
- Use a kanban view for tracking progress.

2. Use Filters to Simplify Views

Apply filters to focus on specific records, such as:

- Tasks assigned to a particular team member.
- Products with low inventory.
- Events happening this week.

3. Organize Views by Purpose

Group similar views together in the sidebar and name them clearly to avoid confusion. For example:

- "Team Tasks: To Do"
- "Marketing Campaigns: Calendar"

4. Use Views to Encourage Collaboration

Create shared views that cater to the needs of different team members. For example, designers might prefer a gallery view, while project managers rely on a timeline view.

Common Challenges and Solutions

Challenge 1: Too Many Views

Having too many views can be overwhelming.

- **Solution**: Consolidate redundant views and delete unused ones.

Challenge 2: Data Overlap Between Views

Sometimes views may display overlapping data.

- **Solution**: Apply distinct filters to each view to ensure they serve unique purposes.

Challenge 3: Confusion Among Team Members

Team members may struggle to identify which view to use.

- **Solution**: Name views descriptively and create a guide to explain their purpose.

Conclusion

Views are a versatile and essential feature of Airtable that allow you to interact with your data in meaningful ways. By understanding and utilizing different view types, you can customize your workflow, improve collaboration, and ensure that your data is presented in the most effective format for each task.

Filtering, Grouping, and Color-Coding

In Airtable, filtering, grouping, and color-coding are essential tools for organizing and visualizing your data effectively. These features allow you to customize how records are displayed within a view, helping you focus on the most relevant information and make your tables more intuitive.

This chapter will walk you through how to apply filters, use grouping to organize records, and leverage color-coding for better data visualization. By the end, you'll have a clear understanding of how to customize your views to suit any workflow.

Filtering Records

Filtering allows you to display only the records that meet specific criteria, hiding everything else. This is especially useful when working with large datasets where only a subset of information is relevant.

How to Apply a Filter

1. Open the table view where you want to apply the filter.
2. Click the **"Filter"** button in the toolbar.
3. Define your filter criteria by selecting a field, a condition, and a value.
   - **Field**: Choose the column you want to filter by.
   - **Condition**: Specify how the field value should be evaluated (e.g., "is," "is not," "contains," "is empty").
   - **Value**: Provide the value the condition will check against.
4. Airtable will instantly filter the records to match your criteria.

Examples of Filters

- Display tasks where the **Status** is "In Progress."
- Show products where the **Stock** is less than 10.
- Highlight events scheduled within the next 7 days using the **Date** field.

Combining Multiple Filters

You can apply multiple filters to refine your results further. Filters can be combined with **AND** or **OR** logic:

- **AND**: Records must meet all filter criteria.
- **OR**: Records must meet at least one of the filter criteria.

Tips for Using Filters

- Save filtered views to quickly access them later.
- Use filters with linked records to display only related data.
- Experiment with conditions like "is empty" or "is not empty" to clean up incomplete records.

Grouping Records

Grouping organizes your records into collapsible stacks based on shared field values. It's an excellent way to visually organize data and identify patterns.

How to Group Records

1. Click the **"Group"** button in the toolbar.

2. Select a field to group by. Airtable will create a stack for each unique value in that field.
    ○ Example: Group tasks by the **Priority** field to separate "High," "Medium," and "Low" priority tasks.
3. To add a second grouping level, click **"Add grouping"** and select another field.

Examples of Grouping

- Group records by **Project** to view all tasks associated with each project.
- Group sales data by **Region** to analyze performance by location.
- Group events by **Month** to organize a calendar of activities.

Customizing Groups

- **Reorder Groups**: Drag and drop groups to rearrange their order.
- **Collapse/Expand Groups**: Click the arrow next to a group to expand or collapse it.
- **Nested Grouping**: Apply multiple grouping levels for detailed organization. For example, group by **Department** first, then by **Team Member**.

Benefits of Grouping

- Quickly identify trends or outliers.
- Simplify navigation in large tables.
- Keep related records organized for better readability.

Color-Coding Records

Color-coding adds a layer of visual distinction to your records, making it easier to identify specific data points at a glance.

How to Add Color-Coding

1. Click the **"Color"** button in the toolbar.
2. Choose to color records based on:
    ○ **Single Select Fields**: Assign a color to each option in a single select field.
    ○ **Conditions**: Define rules to apply colors based on field values or conditions.
3. Select colors for each value or condition from the palette provided.

Examples of Color-Coding

- Assign colors to tasks based on their **Priority** (e.g., red for "High," yellow for "Medium," green for "Low").
- Highlight overdue tasks with a rule that colors records red when the **Due Date** is before today.
- Differentiate projects by assigning unique colors to each **Project Name**.

Advanced Color-Coding Tips

- Use color-coding in combination with filtering and grouping to create highly customized views.
- Apply colors sparingly to avoid overwhelming the table.
- Update color rules as your workflow evolves to maintain relevance.

Combining Filters, Grouping, and Color-Coding

For maximum impact, combine these features to create powerful and intuitive views:

Example 1: Managing Tasks

1. **Filter**: Show only tasks where **Status** is "In Progress."
2. **Group**: Organize tasks by **Project**.
3. **Color-Coding**: Highlight tasks with "High Priority" in red.

Example 2: Analyzing Sales Data

1. **Filter**: Display sales records where the **Revenue** is greater than $10,000.
2. **Group**: Organize by **Salesperson**.
3. **Color-Coding**: Use colors to indicate sales regions (e.g., blue for "North," green for "South").

Example 3: Tracking Events

1. **Filter**: Show only events scheduled in the next 30 days.
2. **Group**: Organize events by **Month**.
3. **Color-Coding**: Assign colors to event types (e.g., workshops, meetings, conferences).

Best Practices for Filtering, Grouping, and Color-Coding

1. **Save Custom Views**
   - Create and save views that combine filters, grouping, and color-coding for specific workflows.
2. **Keep It Simple**
   - Avoid overcomplicating views with too many filters or grouping levels. Focus on what's most relevant.
3. **Update Regularly**
   - Review and adjust your filters, groups, and color rules as your data or priorities change.
4. **Collaborate Effectively**
   - Share custom views with team members to ensure everyone has access to the same organized data.

Common Challenges and Solutions

Challenge 1: Overlapping Filters and Groups

- **Solution**: Test each filter and grouping level individually to ensure they work together as intended.

Challenge 2: Too Many Colors

- **Solution**: Use color-coding sparingly and focus on the most critical distinctions.

Challenge 3: Inconsistent Rules Across Views

- **Solution**: Standardize filter, grouping, and color-coding rules across views used by your team.

Conclusion

Filtering, grouping, and color-coding are powerful tools that bring order to your Airtable bases. By mastering these features, you can customize your views to highlight important data, streamline your workflows, and collaborate more effectively.

Sharing Bases and Permissions

Collaboration is one of Airtable's most powerful features. With its sharing and permission settings, you can invite team members, assign roles, and ensure your data remains secure while enabling seamless teamwork. Whether you're working with a small group or managing a large organization, Airtable provides the flexibility to share bases and set permissions tailored to your workflow.

This chapter will guide you through sharing bases, understanding permission levels, and managing access effectively.

Sharing Your Base

Sharing a base allows others to view or edit your data, depending on the permissions you assign. Airtable makes it easy to collaborate in real time, ensuring everyone stays on the same page.

How to Share a Base

1. **Open the Base**: Navigate to the base you want to share.
2. **Click the Share Button**: In the top-right corner, click the **"Share"** button.
3. **Invite Collaborators**:
    ○ Enter the email addresses of the people you want to invite.
    ○ Assign a permission level to each collaborator (more on permission levels below).
4. **Send the Invite**: Once you've configured permissions, click **"Send invite."**

Sharing with a Link

You can also share a base using a unique link:

1. In the share menu, click **"Create a shareable link."**
2. Choose the permissions for the link:
    ○ **Read-only**: View data without making changes.
    ○ **Allow copying**: Enable others to duplicate the base.
3. Copy and share the link with your team or external stakeholders.

Understanding Permission Levels

Airtable offers granular permission settings to control what collaborators can see and do within a base. This ensures your data stays secure while empowering your team to work effectively.

Permission Levels for Collaborators

1. **Owner**
    ○ Full control over the base, including inviting collaborators, managing permissions, and deleting the base.
    ○ Typically assigned to the creator of the base or a team leader.
2. **Creator**
    ○ Can edit the structure of the base, such as adding fields, tables, and views.
    ○ Can also edit data, invite collaborators, and manage permissions.
3. **Editor**
    ○ Can edit records and data but cannot make structural changes to the base (e.g., adding fields or tables).
    ○ Cannot invite new collaborators or manage permissions.

4. **Commenter**
   - Can view the base and leave comments on records.
   - Cannot edit data or the base structure.
5. **Read-Only**
   - Can view the base but cannot make any changes or leave comments.
   - Ideal for sharing data with external stakeholders who don't need editing access.

Managing Permissions

Permissions can be managed at the base or workspace level, depending on your needs.

Base-Level Permissions

- Use base-level permissions to control access for a specific project or dataset.
- Change a collaborator's permissions by clicking their name in the share menu and selecting a new role.

Workspace-Level Permissions

- Workspace permissions apply to all bases within a workspace.
- Roles include **Owner**, **Creator**, and **Collaborator**, with varying levels of access.

Advanced Permission Settings

For additional security, Airtable offers advanced permission options (available on higher-tier plans):

- **Field Editing Permissions**: Restrict who can edit specific fields.
- **View Access Permissions**: Limit which views collaborators can see.
- **Locked Views**: Prevent collaborators from making changes to a shared view.

Collaborating in Real Time

Once you've shared your base, collaborators can work together in real time. Airtable automatically syncs changes, ensuring everyone sees the latest updates.

Features for Real-Time Collaboration

- **Comments**: Add comments to records and tag collaborators using "@mentions."
- **Activity Log**: Track changes made to records, including who made the changes and when.
- **Revision History**: Restore previous versions of a record if something is accidentally deleted or changed.

Best Practices for Real-Time Collaboration

- Use comments for discussions instead of altering records directly.
- Set clear guidelines for how data should be entered to maintain consistency.
- Regularly review the activity log to monitor changes.

Sharing Bases with External Users

Airtable makes it easy to share data with external users, such as clients or stakeholders, while maintaining control over your base.

Shareable Read-Only Links

- Create a public, read-only link for external users to view your base without needing an Airtable account.
- Customize link settings to allow or restrict copying of the base.

Embedding Views

- Embed a view on a website or intranet using an embed code.
- Ideal for sharing live data with external audiences in a controlled way.

Tips for Managing Shared Bases

1. **Regularly Review Permissions**
   - Periodically review collaborator roles to ensure permissions align with current needs.
   - Remove access for collaborators who no longer need it.
2. **Set View-Specific Permissions**
   - Use locked views or restricted permissions to prevent accidental changes to important data.
3. **Use Clear Naming Conventions**
   - Name views, fields, and bases descriptively so collaborators can navigate easily.
4. **Communicate Expectations**
   - Establish guidelines for how collaborators should interact with the base, such as where to leave comments or how to log changes.
5. **Monitor Activity**
   - Use the activity log to track changes and ensure everyone is following established workflows.

Common Challenges and Solutions

Challenge 1: Over-Sharing Data

- **Solution**: Use read-only links or restricted permissions to limit access to sensitive information.

Challenge 2: Accidental Changes by Collaborators

- **Solution**: Assign appropriate roles (e.g., Read-Only or Commenter) and lock views to prevent structural changes.

Challenge 3: Managing Large Teams

- **Solution**: Set up workspace-level permissions to streamline access for multiple bases. Use groups to manage permissions for teams efficiently.

Conclusion

Sharing bases and managing permissions are critical for effective collaboration in Airtable. By understanding the different permission levels and using advanced sharing features, you can ensure your data is accessible to the right people while maintaining control and security.

Revision History and Collaboration Tips

Effective collaboration is one of Airtable's standout features, and its built-in revision history makes it easy to track changes, recover data, and manage contributions from your team. Whether you're working with a small team or managing a large-scale project, understanding how to use revision history and adopting best practices for collaboration can significantly improve your workflow.

This chapter explores how to utilize Airtable's revision history, manage team dynamics, and foster seamless collaboration.

Understanding Airtable's Revision History

What Is Revision History?

Revision history is a log of all changes made to a base, allowing you to see who made changes, when they occurred, and what was modified. This feature is invaluable for tracking edits, restoring previous versions, and maintaining accountability within your team.

Key Features of Revision History

1. **Record-Level Tracking**
   - View the history of changes for individual records, such as updates to field values or deleted records.
2. **Table-Level Tracking**
   - See a comprehensive log of all changes made within a table.
3. **Collaborator Attribution**
   - Identify which team member made a specific change.
4. **Time Stamps**
   - Review the exact time changes were made for precise tracking.

How to Access Revision History

1. Open the base where you want to review changes.
2. Hover over a record and click the clock icon (**"Activity"**) to view its revision history.
3. For table-level history, click the **"History"** option in the toolbar to see a broader log of changes.

Restoring Previous Versions

If a record is accidentally deleted or an error is made, you can restore a previous version:

1. Open the revision history for the affected record.
2. Locate the desired version using the time stamp.
3. Click **"Restore"** to revert to the earlier state.

Collaboration Tips for Airtable

1. Define Roles and Permissions

Assign appropriate roles to team members to control what they can view and edit:

- **Creators** can modify the structure of a base and invite collaborators.
- **Editors** can modify data but not the base structure.
- **Commenters** can leave feedback without editing.

- **Viewers** have read-only access.

2. Use Comments for Communication

Airtable's commenting feature allows you to discuss changes directly within a record:

- Click the speech bubble icon next to a record to open the comment panel.
- Tag collaborators using "@" to notify them directly.
- Use comments to clarify updates or discuss next steps.

3. Standardize Naming Conventions

Establish consistent naming conventions for fields, records, and views to ensure clarity and avoid confusion. For example:

- Use "Task: [Description]" for task names.
- Prefix views with their purpose, such as "Filtered: High Priority Tasks."

4. Create Shared Views

Provide team members with custom views tailored to their roles or responsibilities. For example:

- A **Kanban view** for tracking progress.
- A **Calendar view** for managing deadlines.
- A **Filtered view** for tasks assigned to specific team members.

5. Lock Critical Views

Prevent accidental changes to important views by locking them:

- Click the view settings menu and enable **"Locked view."**
- Only collaborators with the appropriate permissions can unlock or modify the view.

6. Set Up Notifications

Enable notifications to keep your team informed of changes:

- Use Airtable's built-in notification system to alert collaborators when tasks are updated or completed.
- Integrate with tools like Slack or email for real-time updates.

Managing Collaboration Challenges

Challenge 1: Overlapping Edits

- **Problem**: Multiple team members may edit the same record simultaneously, leading to conflicting changes.
- **Solution**: Use comments to coordinate edits and establish a protocol for handling overlapping tasks.

Challenge 2: Unintentional Changes

- **Problem**: Collaborators may accidentally delete or modify important data.
- **Solution**: Assign roles carefully and regularly monitor the revision history to catch and undo accidental changes.

Challenge 3: Data Entry Errors

- **Problem**: Inconsistent or incorrect data entry disrupts workflows.
- **Solution**: Use predefined field types (e.g., Single Select, Date) to standardize data and minimize errors.

Challenge 4: Lack of Communication

- **Problem**: Team members may not be aware of changes made by others.
- **Solution**: Leverage Airtable's commenting feature and activity log to keep everyone informed.

Advanced Collaboration Tips

1. Use Color-Coding for Clarity

Apply color-coding to highlight tasks, priorities, or responsibilities:

- Example: Use red for overdue tasks, green for completed tasks, and yellow for tasks in progress.

2. Automate Notifications

Set up Airtable Automations to notify collaborators of updates:

- Example: Send an email notification when a task is marked as "Completed."
- Example: Post a Slack message when a new record is added to a table.

3. Leverage Shared Workspaces

For larger teams, organize bases within shared workspaces to centralize access and streamline collaboration.

4. Use Checklists for Consistency

Incorporate checklists into your workflow to standardize processes. For example:

- Add a **Checklist** field to ensure all steps are completed for a task.
- Use a **Single Select** field to track progress through predefined stages.

Best Practices for Team Collaboration

1. **Establish a Workflow**
   - Define a clear workflow for how tasks and data should be managed within the base.
2. **Regularly Review Activity Logs**
   - Periodically check the activity log to monitor changes and ensure accountability.
3. **Provide Training**
   - Train team members on Airtable basics, including how to use comments, filters, and views.
4. **Document Processes**
   - Create documentation or guides for using the base to ensure consistency across the team.

Conclusion: Revision history and collaboration features in Airtable are essential for managing changes, fostering teamwork, and maintaining data accuracy. By understanding how to track changes, restore previous versions, and implement collaboration best practices, you can create an efficient and productive workflow for your team.

Section 4:
Data Linking and Advanced Fields

Linked Records and Rollups

Airtable stands out as a no-code platform because of its ability to link records across tables and aggregate data using rollups. These features allow you to create relationships between tables, making Airtable a powerful relational database. By mastering linked records and rollups, you can streamline workflows, reduce duplicate data, and gain insights from interconnected information.

In this chapter, we'll explore how to set up linked records and rollups, their key use cases, and best practices for building advanced data relationships.

What Are Linked Records?

Linked records allow you to connect related data across tables. Instead of duplicating information, you can create a dynamic link between records in one table and records in another.

How Linked Records Work

When you link records:

- The linked table's data becomes accessible in your current table.
- Updates to linked records are reflected automatically.
- Relationships between data are clearly defined and easy to navigate.

Common Use Cases

- **Project Management**: Link tasks in a "Tasks" table to team members in a "Team Members" table.
- **Customer Relationship Management (CRM)**: Link deals in a "Sales Pipeline" table to customers in a "Clients" table.
- **Event Planning**: Link vendors in a "Vendors" table to events in an "Events" table.

Setting Up Linked Records

Step 1: Add a Linked Record Field

1. Open the table where you want to create the link.
2. Add a new field and select **"Link to another record"** as the field type.
3. Choose the table you want to link to.
   - Example: Link the "Tasks" table to the "Team Members" table.

Step 2: Link Records

1. Click on the linked record field in a row.
2. Select an existing record from the linked table or create a new one.
   - Example: Link a task to a specific team member.
3. The link will appear as a clickable field, allowing you to navigate between related records.

Step 3: Customize Linked Records

- Enable **multiple links** to connect a single record to multiple records in another table.
  - Example: Assign multiple team members to a single task.
- Set up field permissions to control who can create or edit links.

What Are Rollups?

Rollups allow you to aggregate and summarize data from linked records. By combining linked records with rollups, you can perform calculations, generate summaries, and gain deeper insights into your data.

How Rollups Work

Rollups pull data from linked records and apply a formula or aggregation function, such as:

- Summing numbers.
- Finding averages.
- Counting unique values.
- Combining text.

Common Use Cases

- **Project Management**: Calculate total hours worked on a project by summing time entries from linked tasks.
- **Sales Tracking**: Aggregate total revenue from deals linked to a specific client.
- **Inventory Management**: Count total stock across multiple warehouses linked to a product.

Setting Up Rollups

Step 1: Add a Rollup Field

1. Open the table where you want to add the rollup field.
2. Add a new field and select **"Rollup"** as the field type.
3. Choose the linked record field you want to aggregate data from.
   - Example: In a "Projects" table, roll up data from linked "Tasks."

Step 2: Select a Field to Aggregate

1. Choose the specific field in the linked table to aggregate.
   - Example: Select the "Hours Worked" field from linked tasks.

Step 3: Apply an Aggregation Function

1. Choose an aggregation function to apply to the data:
   - **Sum**: Adds numerical values.
   - **Average**: Calculates the mean of numerical values.
   - **Count**: Counts the number of linked records.
   - **ArrayJoin**: Combines text values into a single string.
2. Save the rollup field to display the aggregated result.

Step 4: Use Formulas for Advanced Rollups

Combine rollups with formulas to add conditional logic or perform more complex calculations.

- Example: Use a formula to calculate the percentage of tasks completed in a project.

Benefits of Linked Records and Rollups

1. Eliminate Redundant Data

Linked records ensure that information is stored in one place, reducing duplication and errors.

2. Simplify Data Relationships

Create clear connections between related datasets, making it easier to navigate and analyze data.

3. Automate Summaries and Reports

Rollups provide automated summaries, saving time and ensuring accuracy.

4. Enhance Collaboration

Linked records help teams stay aligned by connecting tasks, resources, and data across tables.

Advanced Tips for Linked Records and Rollups

1. Use Linked Records for Hierarchies

- Create parent-child relationships between tables using linked records.
    - Example: Link a "Projects" table (parent) to a "Tasks" table (child) to track individual tasks under each project.

2. Combine Rollups with Filters

- Use filtered views to limit the records included in rollups.
    - Example: Roll up only the completed tasks from a "Tasks" table.

3. Visualize Relationships with Views

- Create custom views to display relationships clearly, such as grouping tasks by project or team member.

4. Leverage Automations

- Use Airtable Automations to create linked records automatically based on triggers.
    - Example: When a new deal is added to the "Sales Pipeline" table, automatically link it to the corresponding client.

Common Challenges and Solutions

Challenge 1: Too Many Linked Records

- **Problem**: Linking too many records can clutter your tables and make them harder to navigate.
- **Solution**: Use filters and grouping to organize linked records and focus on the most relevant data.

Challenge 2: Inconsistent Links

- **Problem**: Team members may create duplicate or incorrect links.

- **Solution**: Use single select or formula fields to guide consistent linking.

Challenge 3: Misconfigured Rollups

- **Problem**: Rollups may return unexpected results due to incorrect field selection or aggregation functions.
- **Solution**: Double-check the linked record field and the field being aggregated to ensure they match your intent.

Best Practices for Linked Records and Rollups

1. **Keep Tables Focused**
   - Use linked records to separate data into specialized tables rather than combining everything into one table.
2. **Use Descriptive Field Names**
   - Clearly name linked record and rollup fields to indicate their purpose.
   - Example: "Linked Tasks" or "Total Hours Worked."
3. **Test Relationships Before Scaling**
   - Test linked records and rollups with a small dataset before applying them to a large base.
4. **Regularly Review Links and Rollups**
   - Periodically review and update links and rollup fields to ensure they remain accurate and relevant.

Conclusion

Linked records and rollups are two of Airtable's most powerful features, enabling you to build dynamic relationships between tables and gain insights from aggregated data. By using these tools effectively, you can create a relational database tailored to your unique workflows, streamline processes, and unlock the full potential of Airtable.

Lookups and Formula Fields

Lookups and formula fields in Airtable are powerful tools that extend the functionality of your base by enabling advanced data relationships and dynamic calculations. Lookups allow you to retrieve data from linked records, while formula fields let you manipulate data using calculations, logic, and text formatting. Together, these tools enable you to create smart workflows and extract deeper insights from your data.

This chapter will guide you through setting up lookups and formula fields, explain their practical use cases, and offer best practices for using them effectively.

What Are Lookups?

A lookup field retrieves data from a field in a linked table, providing a seamless way to reference related information without duplicating data.

How Lookups Work

When you create a linked record between two tables, a lookup field can pull in additional information from the linked table. For example:

- If you link a "Projects" table to a "Clients" table, a lookup field in the "Projects" table can display the client's email address from the "Clients" table.

Setting Up a Lookup Field

Step 1: Create a Linked Record

Before you can use a lookup field, you need to establish a link between tables.

- Example: Link a "Tasks" table to a "Projects" table.

Step 2: Add a Lookup Field

1. Open the table where you want to add the lookup field.
2. Add a new field and select **"Lookup"** as the field type.
3. Choose the linked record field that connects your table to the other table.
4. Select the field from the linked table that you want to retrieve data from.
   - Example: Pull the "Project Name" field from the "Projects" table into the "Tasks" table.

Step 3: View the Retrieved Data

The lookup field will now display data from the linked table for each record.

Practical Uses for Lookups

1. **Client Management**
   - Link a "Projects" table to a "Clients" table and use a lookup field to display client contact information for each project.
2. **Task Dependencies**
   - In a "Tasks" table, pull in the due date of a dependent task from another table to manage timelines effectively.

3. **Sales Reporting**
   - Link a "Deals" table to a "Sales Reps" table and use a lookup field to display each sales rep's contact details.

What Are Formula Fields?

Formula fields allow you to create dynamic calculations, automate data manipulation, and apply logic to your data. Unlike lookup fields, formula fields work within a single table and do not rely on linked records.

Setting Up a Formula Field

Step 1: Add a Formula Field

1. Open the table where you want to create the formula field.
2. Add a new field and select **"Formula"** as the field type.
3. Enter a formula in the formula editor. Airtable provides a wide range of functions for text, numbers, dates, and logic.
4. Save the field to see the calculated values.

Step 2: Test the Formula

Ensure the formula produces the desired result by testing it with sample data.

Common Formula Functions

1. Text Functions

- **CONCATENATE()**: Combine multiple text fields into one.
  - Example: CONCATENATE({First Name}, " ", {Last Name})
- **UPPER() / LOWER()**: Convert text to uppercase or lowercase.
  - Example: UPPER({Task Name})

2. Number Functions

- **ROUND()**: Round a number to a specified number of decimal places.
  - Example: ROUND({Price}, 2)
- **ABS()**: Return the absolute value of a number.

3. Date Functions

- **DATETIME_DIFF()**: Calculate the difference between two dates.
  - Example: DATETIME_DIFF({Due Date}, TODAY(), "days")
- **DATEADD()**: Add a specific number of days, weeks, or months to a date.
  - Example: DATEADD({Start Date}, 7, "days")

4. Logical Functions

- **IF()**: Apply conditional logic.
  - Example: IF({Status} = "Completed", "✔", "✗")
- **AND() / OR()**: Combine multiple conditions.

    ○ Example: `IF(AND({Priority} = "High", {Due Date} < TODAY())), "Overdue", "On Track")`

5. Aggregation Functions

- **SUM() / AVERAGE()**: Perform calculations across fields.
  - Example: `SUM({Score 1}, {Score 2}, {Score 3})`

Practical Uses for Formula Fields

1. **Automated Status Updates**
   - Use an `IF()` formula to automatically update a status field based on task completion or due dates.
   - Example: `IF({Due Date} < TODAY(), "Overdue", "On Time")`
2. **Combining Names or Titles**
   - Combine first and last names into a single field using `CONCATENATE()`.
   - Example: `CONCATENATE({First Name}, " ", {Last Name})`
3. **Calculating Totals**
   - Sum up numerical values in a table, such as calculating total costs or hours worked.
4. **Conditional Formatting**
   - Use formulas to flag important records.
   - Example: Highlight tasks with high priority using:
     `IF({Priority} = "High", "🔥", "")`

Combining Lookups and Formula Fields

Lookups and formula fields work beautifully together to create dynamic and interconnected workflows.

Example 1: Budget Tracking

- Use a lookup field to pull in a project's budget from a "Projects" table.
- Use a formula field to calculate the remaining budget by subtracting expenses from the total budget.

Example 2: Calculating Completion Percentages

- Use a lookup field to pull in completed task counts from a "Tasks" table.
- Use a formula field to calculate the percentage of tasks completed for a project.

Example 3: Automated Deadlines

- Use a lookup field to pull in start dates from a "Milestones" table.
- Use a formula field with `DATEADD()` to calculate deadlines automatically.

Best Practices for Lookups and Formula Fields

1. **Keep Formulas Simple**
   - Break complex formulas into smaller, manageable parts and test them incrementally.
2. **Use Descriptive Field Names**
   - Clearly name lookup and formula fields to indicate their purpose.

      ○ Example: "Client Email (Lookup)" or "Remaining Budget (Formula)."

3. **Test Formulas Regularly**
    ○ Test formulas with different data scenarios to ensure they work as expected.
4. **Document Complex Relationships**
    ○ Create documentation or guides for lookup and formula setups, especially in shared bases.
5. **Combine Features for Advanced Workflows**
    ○ Experiment with combining lookups, rollups, and formulas to create advanced automation and calculations.

Common Challenges and Solutions

Challenge 1: Formula Errors

- **Problem**: Errors like #ERROR! or unexpected results.
- **Solution**: Double-check syntax and ensure all referenced fields exist and contain valid data.

Challenge 2: Misconfigured Lookups

- **Problem**: Lookup fields not displaying expected data.
- **Solution**: Verify that the linked record field is set up correctly and that records are properly linked.

Challenge 3: Performance Issues

- **Problem**: Complex formulas or excessive lookups slow down the base.
- **Solution**: Optimize formulas and reduce unnecessary fields.

Conclusion

Lookups and formula fields empower you to build smarter, more dynamic bases by connecting data and automating calculations. By mastering these features, you can unlock new levels of efficiency, streamline workflows, and create tailored solutions to fit your needs.

Creating Master-Detail Relationships

Master-detail relationships are a powerful way to structure and organize data in Airtable. This approach enables you to represent hierarchical relationships between tables, such as projects and tasks, clients and invoices, or products and orders. With master-detail relationships, you can create clear connections between overarching categories (masters) and their associated items (details).

This chapter will guide you through setting up master-detail relationships, demonstrate practical use cases, and provide tips for managing these relationships effectively in Airtable.

What Are Master-Detail Relationships?

A **master-detail relationship** links a high-level "master" table to a detailed "child" table.

- **Master Table**: Represents the overarching entity.
    - Example: A "Projects" table.
- **Detail Table**: Represents the individual items associated with each master record.
    - Example: A "Tasks" table where tasks are linked to projects.

By creating this structure, you can keep your data organized, avoid duplication, and enable advanced reporting and automation.

Setting Up Master-Detail Relationships

Step 1: Create Two Tables

1. **Master Table**: Set up the table that represents the overarching entity.
    - Example: A "Projects" table with fields like "Project Name," "Start Date," and "End Date."
2. **Detail Table**: Set up the table that represents the associated items.
    - Example: A "Tasks" table with fields like "Task Name," "Assigned To," and "Due Date."

Step 2: Add a Linked Record Field

1. In the **Detail Table** (e.g., "Tasks"), add a new field and select **"Link to another record"** as the field type.
2. Choose the **Master Table** (e.g., "Projects") to link records.
3. Name the field (e.g., "Project").

Step 3: Link Records

1. In the **Detail Table** (e.g., "Tasks"), click on the linked record field for a row.
2. Select the relevant record from the **Master Table** (e.g., a specific project).
3. Repeat this process for all records that need to be linked.

Adding Rollups to Enhance Relationships

Rollups can be used to aggregate data from the detail table back into the master table, providing summaries or insights.

How to Use Rollups in Master-Detail Relationships

1. In the **Master Table**, add a new field and select **"Rollup"** as the field type.
2. Choose the linked record field that connects the two tables.
3. Select the field from the detail table you want to summarize.
   - Example: Roll up the "Due Date" field from the "Tasks" table to find the latest due date for a project.
4. Apply an aggregation function, such as **SUM**, **AVERAGE**, or **MAX**, to calculate the result.

Practical Use Cases for Master-Detail Relationships

1. Project Management

- **Master Table**: "Projects"
- **Detail Table**: "Tasks"
- Use rollups to calculate the total number of tasks or the percentage of completed tasks for each project.

2. CRM and Sales Pipelines

- **Master Table**: "Clients"
- **Detail Table**: "Deals"
- Link deals to clients and roll up the total deal value to the client record.

3. Inventory Management

- **Master Table**: "Products"
- **Detail Table**: "Orders"
- Track product availability by linking orders to products and rolling up quantities sold.

4. Content Management

- **Master Table**: "Content Categories"
- **Detail Table**: "Articles"
- Organize articles by category and use rollups to count articles per category.

Tips for Managing Master-Detail Relationships

1. Use Clear Naming Conventions

- Name fields and tables clearly to avoid confusion.
  - Example: "Linked Project" instead of "Link."

2. Apply Filters and Views

- Create filtered views in the detail table to display records related to specific master records.
  - Example: Filter tasks to show only those linked to a particular project.

3. Leverage Automations

- Use Airtable Automations to streamline data entry.
  - Example: Automatically create a set of default tasks when a new project is added.

4. Regularly Audit Links

- Periodically review linked records to ensure data accuracy and completeness.

Challenges and Solutions

Challenge 1: Unlinked Records

- **Problem**: Some detail records may not be linked to a master record, causing incomplete relationships.
- **Solution**: Create a filtered view in the detail table to identify unlinked records and update them.

Challenge 2: Managing Many-to-Many Relationships

- **Problem**: A detail record may need to link to multiple master records.
- **Solution**: Enable multiple links in the linked record field or create an intermediate table.
  - Example: Use a "Project-Team Members" table to link team members to multiple projects.

Challenge 3: Overlapping Data

- **Problem**: Redundant data may appear in both the master and detail tables.
- **Solution**: Store shared data in the master table and use lookup fields in the detail table to reference it.

Advanced Techniques for Master-Detail Relationships

1. Conditional Rollups

Use formulas in the detail table to create conditional values that can be rolled up into the master table.

- Example: Add a formula field in the "Tasks" table to calculate whether a task is overdue, and roll up the count of overdue tasks in the "Projects" table.

2. Nested Relationships

Create hierarchies by linking detail tables to additional sub-detail tables.

- Example: Link a "Subtasks" table to a "Tasks" table, which is already linked to a "Projects" table.

3. Linked Field Automations

Set up automations to create linked records automatically based on triggers, such as form submissions or new record creation.

Best Practices for Master-Detail Relationships

1. **Simplify Where Possible**
   - Avoid overly complex relationships by limiting the number of linked tables.
2. **Document Relationships**
   - Create a visual diagram or written documentation to outline how tables and relationships are structured.
3. **Keep Data Clean**
   - Regularly review and clean up unlinked records, duplicate entries, and unused fields.
4. **Test Before Scaling**
   - Test your master-detail setup with a small dataset before applying it to larger workflows.

Conclusion

Master-detail relationships allow you to organize and analyze your data in Airtable with precision and clarity. By linking tables and using rollups to summarize data, you can create a highly functional relational database that adapts to a variety of workflows.

Best Practices for Data Relationships

Establishing effective data relationships in Airtable is critical for building structured, scalable, and intuitive bases. When data is linked and organized well, it becomes easier to analyze, automate, and share insights. However, poorly implemented relationships can lead to errors, inefficiencies, and confusion.

This chapter explores the best practices for creating and managing data relationships in Airtable, ensuring your bases remain functional and optimized as they grow in complexity.

Why Data Relationships Matter

Airtable's power lies in its ability to act as a relational database, connecting information across tables. Data relationships help you:

- **Reduce Redundancy**: Avoid duplicating information across tables by linking related data.
- **Enhance Clarity**: Clearly define how data points relate to one another.
- **Enable Advanced Insights**: Use rollups, lookups, and formulas to gain deeper insights from linked data.
- **Improve Workflow Efficiency**: Streamline workflows by linking related records and automating tasks.

Best Practices for Creating Data Relationships

1. Design Your Base Before Building

Start with a clear plan for how your data will be organized and related. Consider the following questions:

- What entities do you need to track (e.g., tasks, projects, clients)?
- How are these entities related?
- What information needs to be linked between tables?

Example: In a project management base, you might decide to track:

- Projects (Master Table)
- Tasks (Detail Table)
- Team Members (Supporting Table)

2. Use Linked Records for Relationships

Leverage linked record fields to connect related data across tables.

- **Best For**: Creating parent-child relationships, such as linking projects to tasks or clients to invoices.
- Avoid storing the same data in multiple tables; instead, link tables and use lookup fields to reference data.

Example: Link a "Tasks" table to a "Projects" table to associate each task with a specific project.

3. Avoid Overcomplicating Relationships

While it's tempting to create complex relationships, keeping things simple makes your base easier to manage.

- Use separate tables for distinct entities.

- Consolidate data into fewer tables where possible without compromising clarity.

Tip: If a table has too many links, consider whether some relationships could be simplified or removed.

Best Practices for Managing Relationships

1. Use Descriptive Field Names

Clearly name your linked record, lookup, and rollup fields to reflect their purpose.

- Avoid generic names like "Link" or "Data."
- Use descriptive names like "Linked Project" or "Client Email (Lookup)."

2. Establish Naming Conventions

Consistent naming conventions make it easier to understand relationships across tables. Examples include:

- Prefixing linked record fields with "Linked" (e.g., "Linked Client").
- Prefixing lookup fields with "Lookup" (e.g., "Lookup Budget").
- Naming rollup fields based on their calculation (e.g., "Total Hours (Rollup)" or "Average Rating").

3. Leverage Views for Relationship Management

Create custom views to focus on specific relationships:

- **Unlinked Records View**: Filter records that don't have a linked record to ensure all data is properly connected.
- **Grouped Views**: Group records by linked fields to visualize relationships clearly.
  - Example: Group tasks by their linked project.

4. Document Relationships

For complex bases, document how tables are related. This is especially helpful for large teams or collaborative projects.

- Create a diagram or flowchart showing how tables link to one another.
- Include explanations of field purposes and relationships in your base description or a dedicated documentation table.

Optimizing Relationships for Performance

1. Avoid Linking Too Many Records

Linking thousands of records between tables can slow down your base.

- Limit the number of records linked to any single record.
- Archive old records that are no longer relevant.

2. Use Conditional Lookups and Rollups

Filter linked records to focus only on relevant data. For example:

- Use a formula field in the detail table to identify specific conditions (e.g., overdue tasks).
- Roll up only those records that meet the condition.

3. Test Before Scaling

Before applying relationships to a large dataset, test them on a smaller scale to ensure they work as intended.

Advanced Techniques for Data Relationships

1. Many-to-Many Relationships

When an item in one table needs to link to multiple items in another table, create an intermediary table.

- Example: To link team members to multiple projects, create a "Project-Team Members" table with links to both "Projects" and "Team Members."

2. Automating Relationship Management

Use Airtable Automations to create linked records or update relationships automatically.

- **Example**: Automatically link a new task to a project when the project is selected.
- **Example**: Send a notification when a linked record is updated.

3. Use External Tools for Complex Relationships

If your base requires very complex relationships or calculations, consider integrating Airtable with external tools like Zapier or Make (formerly Integromat) for additional processing.

Common Mistakes to Avoid

1. Duplicate Data Across Tables

- **Problem**: Duplicating data increases the risk of inconsistencies.
- **Solution**: Use linked records and lookup fields instead of copying data.

2. Linking Irrelevant Records

- **Problem**: Linking unrelated records clutters your base and makes relationships unclear.
- **Solution**: Establish clear criteria for linking records and regularly review links.

3. Overloading a Single Table

- **Problem**: Storing too many relationships in one table can make it hard to navigate.
- **Solution**: Split data into separate tables and use linked records to connect them.

Best Practices for Collaboration

1. **Assign Ownership**
   - Assign specific team members to manage relationships for each table or set of tables.
2. **Provide Training**
   - Train collaborators on how to create and maintain data relationships.
3. **Restrict Permissions**
   - Limit who can edit linked fields to prevent accidental changes to relationships.
4. **Review Relationships Regularly**

   ○   Periodically audit linked records, lookup fields, and rollups to ensure they remain accurate
       and relevant.

Conclusion

Establishing and maintaining effective data relationships in Airtable is essential for creating organized and
scalable bases. By following these best practices, you can minimize errors, streamline workflows, and
unlock the full potential of Airtable's relational database features.

Section 5:
Using Forms for Data Collection

Designing Forms in Airtable

Forms are one of Airtable's most versatile features, enabling you to collect data directly into your base from internal or external users. Whether you're gathering customer feedback, creating surveys, or managing event registrations, Airtable's form view offers a simple yet powerful way to streamline data collection.

This chapter will walk you through the process of designing forms in Airtable, covering customization options, best practices, and real-world examples to help you get the most out of this feature.

What Are Airtable Forms?

Forms in Airtable allow you to collect information directly into a table by presenting selected fields in an intuitive, user-friendly interface. Once submitted, the data automatically creates a new record in the corresponding table, ensuring seamless integration with your existing workflows.

Setting Up a Form in Airtable

Step 1: Create a Form View

1. Open the table where you want to collect data.
2. Click the **"+"** button next to the views section in the sidebar.
3. Select **"Form"** as the view type and name your form.

Step 2: Select and Arrange Fields

1. Airtable will automatically include all fields from the table in the form. You can customize which fields to include by toggling their visibility.
2. Drag and drop fields to rearrange their order in the form.

Step 3: Customize Field Settings

- **Field Labels**: Edit field labels to provide clear instructions or context.
- **Required Fields**: Mark important fields as required to ensure users provide the necessary information.
- **Default Values**: Set default values for fields where applicable.
- **Field Types**: Use appropriate field types (e.g., Single Select, Date, Attachment) to guide users and maintain data consistency.

Step 4: Add a Title and Description

1. Add a title to your form that reflects its purpose.
2. Include a description to provide context, instructions, or additional details for users.

Customizing Your Form

Branding and Visual Design

While Airtable forms have a clean and minimalistic design by default, you can customize their appearance to align with your branding:

- Add a **logo** or header image to personalize the form.
- Use descriptive field names and organized layouts to enhance usability.

Form Behavior Settings

1. **Allow Multiple Submissions**: Choose whether users can submit the form multiple times.
2. **Show a Confirmation Message**: Customize the message users see after submitting the form.
3. **Redirect After Submission**: Redirect users to a specific URL (e.g., a thank-you page) after they complete the form.

Sharing Your Form

1. Click the **"Share Form"** button in the top-right corner of the form view.
2. Share the form using a unique URL, or embed it directly on your website.

Best Practices for Designing Airtable Forms

1. Keep It Simple

- Only include the fields necessary for the form's purpose.
- Use clear and concise labels to make the form easy to understand.

2. Group Related Fields

- Arrange fields logically to create a smooth user experience.
- For example, group personal information fields (e.g., name, email) at the top, followed by details related to the submission.

3. Use Conditional Fields

- While Airtable does not natively support conditional logic, you can manually hide fields that may not apply to all users. Alternatively, use third-party tools like JotForm or Typeform with Airtable integrations for advanced conditional logic.

4. Test Your Form

- Submit test entries to ensure the form functions as intended.
- Check that required fields are enforced, default values are accurate, and submitted data flows correctly into your base.

5. Optimize for Mobile Devices

- Airtable forms are mobile-friendly by default, but test your form on different devices to ensure it remains easy to use.

Real-World Use Cases for Airtable Forms

1. Event Registration

- Use a form to collect attendee information, such as name, email, and dietary preferences.
- Link the form to an "Events" table to manage RSVPs and attendance.

2. Customer Feedback

- Create a form to gather customer feedback on products or services.
- Include fields for ratings, comments, and suggestions.

3. Lead Capture

- Embed a form on your website to capture leads.
- Include fields for name, email, company, and interest areas, and link it to your CRM table.

4. Job Applications

- Build a form for job applicants to submit resumes and cover letters.
- Use attachment fields to collect files and link applications to a "Candidates" table.

5. Internal Task Requests

- Create a form for team members to request tasks or resources.
- Include fields for task description, priority level, and due date.

Advanced Features

Integrating Forms with Automations

- Use Airtable Automations to trigger actions when a form is submitted.
  - Example: Send an email notification to a team member when a new submission is received.

Embedding Forms on Websites

- Copy the embed code from the form's sharing settings to display the form on your website or intranet.

Third-Party Form Builders

- For advanced customization, use third-party tools like Google Forms, JotForm, or Typeform, and integrate them with Airtable using tools like Zapier or Make (formerly Integromat).

Common Challenges and Solutions

Challenge 1: Users Skipping Important Fields

- **Solution**: Mark critical fields as required to ensure users provide necessary information.

Challenge 2: Cluttered Form Design

- **Solution**: Remove unnecessary fields and group related fields to improve readability.

Challenge 3: Limited Customization Options

- **Solution**: Use third-party form builders for advanced styling and logic while integrating them with Airtable.

Conclusion

Designing forms in Airtable is a straightforward and powerful way to collect data from users while seamlessly integrating it into your base. By following the best practices outlined in this chapter, you can create forms that are user-friendly, efficient, and tailored to your specific needs.

Managing Form Responses

Once you've designed and shared a form in Airtable, managing the responses effectively is the next crucial step. Airtable makes it easy to process, organize, and analyze the data collected through forms by integrating responses directly into your base. With features like filtering, grouping, and automation, you can streamline your workflow and ensure your data is actionable.

This chapter explores how to manage form responses efficiently, provides tips for organizing your data, and outlines best practices for keeping your base clean and functional.

How Form Responses Work in Airtable

Form responses are added to the table as new records, with each submitted form creating a single record. Each field in the form corresponds to a field in the table, and the data entered by the user is populated automatically.

Features of Airtable Form Responses

- **Real-Time Updates**: Responses appear instantly in your table, eliminating the need for manual data entry.
- **Customizable Fields**: Fields in the table can be configured to automatically process or categorize responses.
- **Integration with Views**: Responses can be filtered, grouped, and sorted within views for better organization.

Organizing Form Responses

1. Create a Dedicated View for Responses

To make it easier to manage and review responses, create a new view specifically for form submissions:

- **Filtered View**: Show only the records created through form submissions.
- **Grouped View**: Group responses by key fields, such as submission date, category, or priority.
- **Sorted View**: Sort responses based on criteria like timestamps or specific fields.

2. Add a Timestamp Field

Include a **Created Time** field in your table to automatically capture the date and time of each submission. This helps track when responses were received and prioritize follow-ups.

3. Use Single Select Fields for Categorization

For forms with open-ended responses, use single select fields to manually or automatically categorize submissions.

- Example: Categorize customer feedback into "Positive," "Neutral," or "Negative."

4. Assign Ownership to Responses

Add a collaborator field to assign responses to team members. This is particularly useful for task delegation or follow-ups.

Reviewing and Processing Responses

1. Identify Incomplete Submissions

Use filters to identify responses with missing or incomplete data:

- Example: Filter for records where required fields (e.g., "Email" or "Phone Number") are empty.

2. Validate Data

Review form responses for accuracy and consistency. If necessary, use validation rules to ensure data integrity:

- **Predefined Field Types**: Use email, date, or single select fields to standardize inputs.
- **Automation Rules**: Create automations to flag or notify you of invalid entries.

3. Follow Up on Submissions

For responses that require follow-up, create a checklist or add a "Follow-Up Status" field to track progress.

- Example: Use single select options like "Pending," "In Progress," and "Completed."

Automating Response Management

1. Send Notifications for New Responses

Use Airtable Automations to notify team members of new submissions:

- **Email Notifications**: Send an email to the appropriate person or team when a new response is submitted.
- **Slack Notifications**: Post updates to a Slack channel for real-time collaboration.

2. Update Fields Automatically

Set up automations to update fields based on specific conditions:

- Example: Automatically assign new submissions to a team member based on their category.

3. Create Follow-Up Records

Automatically generate related records in other tables based on form submissions:

- Example: When a customer feedback form is submitted, create a follow-up task in a "Tasks" table.

Analyzing Form Responses

1. Use Rollups and Lookups

- Roll up responses to analyze trends, such as the number of submissions by category or average response ratings.
- Use lookup fields to connect responses to related data, such as linking feedback to specific products or services.

2. Visualize Data with Charts

Use Airtable's chart blocks (or integrate with tools like Google Data Studio or Tableau) to visualize form response data:

- Example: Create a pie chart showing the distribution of responses by category.
- Example: Generate a bar graph of submission volume over time.

3. Export Data for Further Analysis

If needed, export your form responses to analyze them in external tools like Excel or Python:

1. Go to your table.
2. Click the **"Download CSV"** option to export the data.

Real-World Use Cases for Managing Form Responses

1. Event Registration

- Automatically group responses by event name or registration type.
- Use rollups to calculate total registrations or available slots.
- Assign follow-up tasks to team members for incomplete or flagged responses.

2. Customer Feedback

- Categorize feedback into themes (e.g., product features, pricing, support).
- Create follow-up tasks for critical feedback.
- Use charts to identify recurring issues or highly praised aspects.

3. Job Applications

- Filter applications by job role or experience level.
- Assign applications to recruiters for review.
- Use automations to send confirmation emails to applicants.

4. Internal Requests

- Group requests by department or urgency level.
- Assign tasks to the appropriate teams or individuals.
- Track completion status using a "Request Status" field.

Common Challenges and Solutions

Challenge 1: Duplicate Submissions

- **Problem**: Users may submit the form multiple times.
- **Solution**: Use filters to identify and merge duplicates or add a unique identifier field, such as an email address.

Challenge 2: Missing Data

- **Problem**: Incomplete submissions may reduce the usefulness of the data.
- **Solution**: Make essential fields required in the form to ensure completeness.

Challenge 3: Overwhelming Volume of Responses

- **Problem**: Managing large volumes of responses can become challenging.

- **Solution**: Use filters, grouping, and automation to prioritize and streamline processing.

Best Practices for Managing Form Responses

1. **Keep Your Base Organized**
   - Use views, filters, and field types to maintain clarity and focus.
2. **Regularly Review and Update Data**
   - Periodically audit your table to correct errors and remove outdated records.
3. **Collaborate Effectively**
   - Assign responses to team members and communicate updates using comments or notifications.
4. **Integrate with Other Tools**
   - Use integrations with Slack, email, or third-party apps to enhance your workflow.
5. **Analyze Trends Over Time**
   - Use Airtable's charting tools or external analytics platforms to track trends and measure impact.

Conclusion

Managing form responses effectively is key to unlocking the full potential of Airtable's form feature. By organizing, validating, and analyzing responses, you can turn raw data into actionable insights and streamline your workflows.

Embedding Forms on Websites

Embedding Airtable forms on a website is a powerful way to collect data from external users, such as customers, partners, or event attendees. By integrating forms directly into your website, you can gather information seamlessly while maintaining a professional and user-friendly experience. This chapter will guide you through the process of embedding Airtable forms on websites, customizing their appearance, and ensuring they fit your workflow.

Why Embed Forms on a Website?

Embedding forms on a website provides several benefits:

- **Accessibility**: Make forms easily accessible to a wider audience.
- **Seamless Data Collection**: Responses are automatically added to your Airtable base, reducing manual data entry.
- **Customization**: Integrate forms into your website's design and branding for a cohesive user experience.
- **Real-Time Updates**: Allow data collection in real-time, ensuring timely insights.

Steps to Embed an Airtable Form

Step 1: Design Your Form

Before embedding, ensure your form is ready to go:

1. Create a form view in your Airtable base (refer to Chapter 17 for detailed instructions).
2. Customize the form fields, title, and description to fit the purpose of the form.
3. Test the form by submitting sample entries to confirm functionality.

Step 2: Generate the Embed Code

1. Open the form view in Airtable.
2. Click the **"Share Form"** button in the top-right corner.
3. In the sharing options, select **"Embed this form on your site"** to generate the embed code.
4. Copy the HTML embed code provided.

Step 3: Add the Embed Code to Your Website

1. Open your website's content management system (CMS) or HTML editor.
2. Navigate to the page where you want the form to appear.
3. Paste the embed code into the appropriate section of your page (e.g., a text editor, HTML block, or custom code area).
4. Save and preview your page to ensure the form displays correctly.

Customizing the Embedded Form

While Airtable forms have a clean, default design, you can customize their appearance to better match your website's branding and layout.

Customizations Within Airtable

1. **Form Header**: Add a logo or image to the form header to personalize it.
2. **Field Labels**: Ensure field names and descriptions are clear and concise.
3. **Confirmation Message**: Customize the post-submission message to thank users or provide next steps.

Customizations Using Website Tools

Depending on your website platform, you may have additional customization options:

- **Resize the Form**: Adjust the width and height of the embed code to ensure the form fits your webpage layout.
- **Style the Form Container**: Use CSS to apply custom fonts, colors, or borders to the form's container.
- **Mobile Optimization**: Test the form's appearance on mobile devices and adjust the size or alignment if needed.

Embedding Forms on Popular Website Platforms

1. WordPress

1. Use the WordPress block editor (Gutenberg) or a page builder like Elementor.
2. Add a custom HTML block to your page or post.
3. Paste the embed code and save your changes.

2. Squarespace

1. Open the page editor in Squarespace.
2. Add a **Code Block** to your page.
3. Paste the embed code into the Code Block and save.

3. Wix

1. Open the Wix Editor and select the page where you want the form.
2. Add an **HTML Embed** element from the toolbar.
3. Paste the embed code and adjust the size and position.

4. Shopify

1. Open the theme editor for your Shopify store.
2. Add a new section or edit an existing one.
3. Insert the embed code into the HTML area and save.

Best Practices for Embedding Airtable Forms

1. Match the Form Design to Your Website

- Use similar fonts, colors, and button styles to create a cohesive experience.
- Add a header image or logo to align with your brand identity.

2. Test the Form on All Devices

- Check the form's functionality and appearance on desktops, tablets, and smartphones.
- Ensure the form fields are easy to interact with on smaller screens.

3. Use HTTPS for Secure Embedding

- Ensure your website uses HTTPS to maintain security and avoid browser warnings.

4. Optimize the Form's Placement

- Position the form where it's easy for users to find, such as above the fold or near relevant content.
- Avoid cluttering the page with too many elements around the form.

5. Provide Clear Instructions

- Add brief instructions or examples for each field to guide users through the form.

6. Track Form Performance

- Use Airtable's timestamp field to track submission frequency.
- Integrate with tools like Google Analytics to monitor form engagement on your website.

Advanced Use Cases

1. Embedding Forms for Lead Capture

- Use Airtable forms on your website's landing pages to collect lead information, such as name, email, and interest areas.
- Automate follow-ups by integrating Airtable with email marketing tools like Mailchimp or ActiveCampaign.

2. Event Registration

- Embed a registration form for webinars, workshops, or conferences.
- Use Airtable to track RSVPs, send reminders, and manage attendance.

3. Customer Feedback

- Add a feedback form to your website to collect user suggestions, testimonials, or complaints.
- Categorize feedback automatically in your Airtable base for analysis.

4. Product Inquiries

- Embed a product inquiry form on e-commerce product pages.
- Link the form to your inventory or customer support base to manage responses.

Troubleshooting Common Issues

Issue 1: Form Doesn't Display Correctly

- **Solution**: Check that the embed code was copied and pasted correctly. Ensure your website supports iframe embeds.

Issue 2: Form Not Responsive on Mobile

- **Solution**: Adjust the width and height parameters in the embed code. Add CSS to make the form container responsive.

Issue 3: Submissions Not Appearing in Airtable

- **Solution**: Verify that the form is linked to the correct table and that fields are mapped correctly. Test the form with a sample submission.

Conclusion

Embedding Airtable forms on your website enables seamless data collection while maintaining a professional and user-friendly experience. By customizing and optimizing your forms, you can ensure they align with your brand and serve your specific needs.

Streamlining Form-Based Workflows

Creating forms in Airtable is just the beginning of efficient data collection. To truly maximize the value of your forms, you need to establish streamlined workflows that make it easy to process, analyze, and act on the collected data. By automating repetitive tasks, integrating with external tools, and organizing responses effectively, you can create a seamless pipeline from form submission to actionable outcomes.

This chapter will guide you through the strategies and tools to streamline form-based workflows in Airtable, ensuring efficiency and productivity for your team.

The Benefits of Streamlined Workflows

Streamlined workflows reduce manual effort, improve data accuracy, and ensure timely follow-up. Key advantages include:

- **Efficiency**: Automate routine tasks like notifications, data categorization, and task creation.
- **Consistency**: Ensure uniform data processing and eliminate errors.
- **Scalability**: Handle a growing volume of form responses without additional effort.

Automating Form Responses

Automation is at the heart of streamlining workflows in Airtable. Automations enable you to trigger specific actions when a form response is received.

1. Send Notifications

Notify the appropriate person or team whenever a form is submitted.

- **How to Set Up**:
    - Open the Automations tab in your Airtable base.
    - Create a new automation and select **"When a record is created"** as the trigger.
    - Add an action, such as sending an email or posting to a Slack channel.
- **Example**:
    - Notify your customer support team when a feedback form is submitted.
    - Send a thank-you email to the respondent automatically.

2. Assign Tasks Automatically

Use automations to assign tasks based on form responses.

- **How to Set Up**:
    - Add a collaborator field to your table.
    - Use an automation to assign a team member based on a field value (e.g., category or priority).
- **Example**:
    - Assign sales inquiries to specific team members based on the region selected in the form.

3. Categorize Submissions Automatically

Set up conditional logic to categorize form responses.

- **How to Set Up**:
    - Use a single select or formula field to categorize submissions.

    ○ Create an automation to update the field based on specific criteria.
- **Example**:
  - ○ Tag feedback as "Positive," "Neutral," or "Negative" based on sentiment keywords.

Integrating Airtable Forms with External Tools

Airtable forms become even more powerful when integrated with other tools. Use integrations to create a seamless workflow across platforms.

1. Integrating with Email Tools

- **Use Case**: Send follow-up emails after form submissions.
- **Tools**: Zapier, Make (formerly Integromat), or Airtable Automations.
- **Example**: Send a personalized email via Mailchimp when a new lead form is submitted.

2. Integrating with Project Management Tools

- **Use Case**: Convert form submissions into tasks in tools like Asana, Trello, or ClickUp.
- **Tools**: Zapier or Make.
- **Example**: Create a new Trello card for each event registration submitted via Airtable.

3. Connecting with CRM Systems

- **Use Case**: Add new form submissions directly to your CRM.
- **Tools**: Salesforce, HubSpot, or Pipedrive integrations via Zapier or native connectors.
- **Example**: Add new leads from an Airtable form to your HubSpot CRM and trigger a sales sequence.

4. Syncing with Google Workspace

- **Use Case**: Add form submissions to Google Sheets for reporting or create calendar events based on responses.
- **Tools**: Google Workspace integrations via Zapier or Make.
- **Example**: Add new form submissions to a Google Sheet for detailed reporting and analysis.

Organizing Form Responses

Effective organization is key to ensuring form responses are actionable.

1. Use Views to Filter and Sort Responses

- **Filtered Views**: Show only records that meet specific criteria, such as high-priority submissions.
- **Grouped Views**: Group responses by fields like category, submission date, or status.
- **Sorted Views**: Sort records to prioritize actions, such as earliest deadlines or most urgent tasks.

2. Add Status Tracking

Include a single select or checkbox field to track the status of each response.

- **Examples**:
  - ○ "Pending," "In Progress," "Completed."
  - ○ Use a checkbox for "Follow-Up Required."

3. Archive Old Responses

Move older or completed responses to an archive table to keep your main table clean and focused.

Advanced Techniques for Streamlining Workflows

1. Conditional Logic in Form Responses

Although Airtable forms don't natively support conditional fields, you can use automations or formulas to replicate this functionality:

- **Example**: Use a formula field to apply conditional logic, such as calculating urgency based on the due date.

2. Use Linked Tables for Complex Workflows

Link form responses to other tables for more advanced workflows:

- **Example**: Link feedback forms to a "Product Features" table to analyze which features are most requested.

3. Generate Reports Automatically

Use Airtable's chart blocks or integrate with tools like Google Data Studio to create automated reports based on form submissions.

4. Create Templates for Follow-Ups

Standardize your follow-up process by creating templates for common responses or actions.

- **Example**: Use a predefined email template for customer inquiries.

Real-World Use Cases

1. Customer Support Tickets

- **Form**: Collect support tickets from customers.
- **Workflow**:
    - Automatically assign tickets to support agents based on category.
    - Notify the agent via email or Slack.
    - Track ticket status and completion in Airtable.

2. Event Management

- **Form**: Gather event registrations.
- **Workflow**:
    - Send a confirmation email to attendees.
    - Add attendees to an event logistics table.
    - Generate a checklist for follow-up tasks after the event.

3. Internal Requests

- **Form**: Collect internal resource or task requests from team members.
- **Workflow**:
    - Route requests to the appropriate department based on form inputs.
    - Track progress and approvals in Airtable.

Common Challenges and Solutions

Challenge 1: Overwhelmed by Submissions

- **Problem**: High submission volume makes it difficult to process responses.
- **Solution**: Use filters, automations, and integrations to prioritize and delegate tasks.

Challenge 2: Inconsistent Data

- **Problem**: Responses contain errors or inconsistencies.
- **Solution**: Use field validation and predefined field types to ensure accurate data entry.

Challenge 3: Delayed Follow-Ups

- **Problem**: Manual processes delay follow-ups.
- **Solution**: Automate notifications and task assignments to ensure timely responses.

Best Practices for Streamlining Form-Based Workflows

1. **Automate Repetitive Tasks**
   - Use Airtable Automations or integrations to handle routine actions.
2. **Test Workflows Before Scaling**
   - Pilot workflows with a small dataset to ensure everything functions as expected.
3. **Regularly Review Processes**
   - Periodically evaluate your workflows to identify areas for improvement.
4. **Train Your Team**
   - Ensure all team members understand how to use Airtable and the workflows in place.

Conclusion

Streamlining form-based workflows in Airtable enables you to handle data collection, organization, and action with ease. By leveraging automations, integrations, and best practices, you can transform form responses into actionable insights and ensure your processes remain efficient as your needs grow.

Section 6:
Automations and Integrations

Introduction to Airtable Automations

Airtable Automations is one of the platform's most powerful features, enabling you to automate repetitive tasks and create efficient workflows without writing code. By setting up triggers and actions, you can streamline processes, reduce manual effort, and ensure consistency in your data management.

In this chapter, we'll explore what Airtable Automations are, how they work, and how you can start leveraging them to optimize your Airtable bases.

What Are Airtable Automations?

Automations in Airtable are workflows that run automatically when specific conditions are met. Each automation consists of two components:

1. **Trigger**: The event that starts the automation (e.g., when a record is created or updated).
2. **Action**: The task that is performed automatically (e.g., sending an email, updating a field, or creating a new record).

With automations, you can eliminate repetitive tasks, such as notifying team members of updates, generating reports, or integrating Airtable with external apps and services.

Key Features of Airtable Automations

1. Triggers

Triggers define the event that starts the automation. Airtable offers a variety of triggers, including:

- **When a record is created**: Starts the automation when a new record is added to a table.
- **When a record is updated**: Starts the automation when specific fields in a record are modified.
- **At a scheduled time**: Runs the automation on a recurring schedule (e.g., daily or weekly).

2. Actions

Actions define what happens after the trigger. Airtable provides a wide range of built-in actions, including:

- **Update record**: Modify fields in an existing record.
- **Send an email**: Notify someone via email.
- **Create record**: Add a new record to a table.
- **Send a Slack message**: Post a message to a Slack channel.

3. External Integrations

Airtable Automations can integrate with popular third-party tools and services, including Gmail, Slack, Outlook, and more, allowing you to extend the functionality of your workflows.

Why Use Airtable Automations?

1. Save Time

Automations reduce the time spent on repetitive tasks, freeing you to focus on more strategic work.

2. Ensure Consistency

By automating processes, you can ensure tasks are performed consistently and accurately every time.

3. Improve Collaboration

Automatically notify team members of updates, assignments, or upcoming deadlines to keep everyone on the same page.

4. Boost Productivity

Streamline workflows by eliminating bottlenecks and enabling faster decision-making.

Setting Up Your First Automation

Step 1: Open the Automations Tab

1. Open the Airtable base where you want to set up the automation.
2. Click the **"Automations"** tab at the top of the interface.

Step 2: Add a New Automation

1. Click **"Create an automation"** to start building a new workflow.
2. Name your automation to reflect its purpose (e.g., "Send Notification for New Tasks").

Step 3: Choose a Trigger

1. Select a trigger type from the list (e.g., "When a record is created").
2. Configure the trigger settings, such as selecting the table and conditions (if applicable).

Step 4: Add an Action

1. Select an action type (e.g., "Send an email").
2. Configure the action settings, such as recipient, subject, and message content.
3. Use dynamic values from your table (e.g., fields like name or email) to personalize the action.

Step 5: Test the Automation

1. Click **"Test trigger"** to verify that the trigger works as expected.
2. Test the action to ensure the desired result is achieved (e.g., sending a test email).

Step 6: Turn On the Automation

1. Once the automation is set up and tested, toggle it **on** to activate it.
2. Monitor the automation's activity to ensure it runs correctly.

Common Use Cases for Airtable Automations

1. Task Notifications

- **Trigger**: When a task is assigned to a team member.
- **Action**: Send an email or Slack message notifying them of the assignment.

2. Lead Management

- **Trigger**: When a new lead is added to a "Leads" table.
- **Action**: Automatically send a welcome email or add the lead to your CRM system.

3. Approval Workflows

- **Trigger**: When a record's status changes to "Pending Approval."
- **Action**: Notify the approver and create a task for the review.

4. Data Cleanup

- **Trigger**: When a record is missing a required field.
- **Action**: Update the record with default values or notify a team member to fill in the missing data.

Best Practices for Using Automations

1. Start Simple

Begin with basic automations to get comfortable with the process. Gradually add more complexity as needed.

2. Test Thoroughly

Always test your automations to ensure they work as intended. Check both the trigger and action steps.

3. Use Descriptive Names

Give your automations clear and descriptive names to easily identify their purpose.

4. Monitor Automation Logs

Review the automation logs regularly to track activity and troubleshoot any issues.

5. Avoid Overloading Automations

Keep automations focused and specific to prevent conflicts or unintended actions.

Limitations of Airtable Automations

While Airtable Automations are incredibly useful, it's important to be aware of their limitations:

- **Run Limits**: Free and paid plans have limits on the number of automation runs per month.
- **Complex Logic**: Airtable Automations don't natively support advanced conditional logic (e.g., if-else statements). For complex workflows, consider integrating with tools like Zapier or Make.
- **Execution Time**: Automations may experience delays during peak usage times.

Expanding Automations with External Tools

For more advanced workflows, you can integrate Airtable Automations with external tools:

- **Zapier**: Connect Airtable with over 5,000 apps to create multi-step workflows.
- **Make (formerly Integromat)**: Design complex automation scenarios with advanced logic and branching.
- **Custom Scripts**: Use scripting blocks within Airtable to create bespoke actions tailored to your needs.

Conclusion

Airtable Automations unlock a new level of efficiency and productivity by reducing manual effort and streamlining workflows. Whether you're sending notifications, managing tasks, or integrating with external tools, automations can help you get more done with less effort.

Setting Up Automated Triggers

Automated triggers are the backbone of Airtable's automation capabilities. Triggers define the events that initiate automated workflows, allowing you to set processes into motion without manual intervention. Whether you want to send notifications, update records, or integrate with external tools, setting up triggers is the first step to streamlining your workflows.

In this chapter, we'll explore how to configure automated triggers in Airtable, provide examples of common use cases, and share best practices to ensure your automations run efficiently.

What Are Automated Triggers?

A trigger is the event that starts an automation. It monitors your base for specific changes or occurrences and activates the associated action when the criteria are met. Airtable offers a variety of triggers, making it easy to customize workflows to suit your needs.

Types of Automated Triggers in Airtable

Airtable provides several trigger types, each designed to accommodate different workflows:

1. When a Record Is Created

- **Description**: Activates when a new record is added to a table.
- **Use Case**: Notify team members when a new task or lead is added.

2. When a Record Is Updated

- **Description**: Activates when specific fields in a record are modified.
- **Use Case**: Trigger follow-up actions when a status field changes to "Completed" or "Pending Approval."

3. When a Record Matches Conditions

- **Description**: Activates when a record meets defined conditions, such as specific field values.
- **Use Case**: Send reminders for overdue tasks or flag records with missing data.

4. At a Scheduled Time

- **Description**: Runs the automation at a specific time or on a recurring schedule.
- **Use Case**: Generate daily reports or send weekly reminders.

5. When a Form Is Submitted

- **Description**: Activates when a form is submitted and creates a new record.
- **Use Case**: Send a thank-you email or assign follow-up tasks after receiving form submissions.

Setting Up Automated Triggers

Step 1: Open the Automations Tab

1. Navigate to the Airtable base where you want to create the automation.
2. Click on the **"Automations"** tab in the toolbar at the top.

Step 2: Create a New Automation

1. Click **"Create an automation."**
2. Name your automation to reflect its purpose (e.g., "Notify Team of New Leads").

Step 3: Select a Trigger

1. Choose a trigger type from the list of available options.
2. Configure the trigger settings based on your workflow requirements:
    ○ **For record-based triggers**: Select the table and conditions to monitor.
    ○ **For scheduled triggers**: Define the date, time, and frequency.

Step 4: Test the Trigger

1. Click **"Test trigger"** to verify that it works as expected.
2. If the trigger finds a matching record or event, the test will return the details for review.

Examples of Automated Triggers

1. Lead Management

- **Trigger**: When a new record is created in the "Leads" table.
- **Action**: Automatically send an email to the sales team with the lead's details.

2. Task Tracking

- **Trigger**: When a record in the "Tasks" table is updated to "Completed."
- **Action**: Notify the project manager and mark the project as "In Progress" if all tasks are completed.

3. Event Registration

- **Trigger**: When a form submission creates a new record in the "Registrations" table.
- **Action**: Send a confirmation email to the registrant and add them to a mailing list.

4. Scheduled Reporting

- **Trigger**: At 8:00 AM every Monday.
- **Action**: Generate a weekly progress report and send it to stakeholders.

Advanced Trigger Configurations

1. Using Conditional Triggers

- Combine triggers with filters to activate automations only under specific conditions.
- Example: Trigger an automation only when the "Priority" field is set to "High" and the "Due Date" is within 3 days.

2. Monitoring Multiple Tables

- Use separate automations to trigger actions across different tables and link them for a cohesive workflow.
- Example: Trigger one automation when a task is completed in the "Tasks" table, which then updates a related record in the "Projects" table.

3. Combining Triggers with External Tools

- Integrate triggers with tools like Zapier or Make (formerly Integromat) to expand functionality.
- Example: Use a trigger to notify Slack and update a Google Sheet simultaneously.

Common Challenges and Solutions

Challenge 1: Trigger Doesn't Activate

- **Cause**: The trigger conditions are too restrictive or improperly set.
- **Solution**: Double-check the conditions and test the trigger to ensure it's correctly configured.

Challenge 2: Automation Runs Too Frequently

- **Cause**: Triggers are overly broad or not specific enough.
- **Solution**: Add filters to narrow down the trigger conditions.

Challenge 3: Overlapping Automations

- **Cause**: Multiple automations are triggered by the same event.
- **Solution**: Consolidate related automations or adjust trigger settings to avoid conflicts.

Best Practices for Setting Up Triggers

1. Use Descriptive Trigger Names

Clearly name your triggers to reflect their purpose and avoid confusion when managing multiple automations.

2. Test Regularly

Test your triggers frequently to ensure they work correctly, especially after making changes to your base or automation setup.

3. Monitor Automation Logs

Review the automation logs in Airtable to track activity, identify issues, and make adjustments as needed.

4. Avoid Overlapping Conditions

Ensure that triggers are distinct and don't overlap, which could result in duplicate or conflicting actions.

5. Optimize Trigger Settings

Keep triggers as specific as possible to minimize unnecessary runs and improve efficiency.

Conclusion

Setting up automated triggers in Airtable is the first step toward creating powerful, streamlined workflows. By understanding the different types of triggers and how to configure them effectively, you can automate repetitive tasks, improve data consistency, and save time.

Integrating with Third-Party Services

Airtable's ability to integrate with third-party services is one of its most powerful features, enabling you to create seamless workflows that connect Airtable to your favorite tools. From email marketing platforms to project management software, integrating Airtable allows you to expand its functionality, automate processes, and centralize data across systems.

In this chapter, we'll explore the benefits of integrating Airtable with third-party services, provide step-by-step instructions for common integrations, and share best practices for setting up efficient workflows.

Why Integrate Airtable with Other Tools?

Integrations allow you to:

- **Centralize Data**: Sync information between Airtable and other platforms to maintain a single source of truth.
- **Automate Processes**: Eliminate manual tasks by automating workflows across multiple apps.
- **Enhance Functionality**: Extend Airtable's capabilities with specialized tools for email, analytics, or project management.
- **Improve Collaboration**: Share data and updates between teams using different systems.

Methods for Integrating Airtable with Third-Party Services

There are multiple ways to connect Airtable with other tools, depending on your workflow requirements and technical expertise.

1. Native Integrations

Airtable offers built-in integrations with popular tools like Slack, Gmail, and Outlook, which can be accessed directly through Airtable Automations.

- **Example**: Send an email via Gmail when a record is updated.

2. Integration Platforms

Third-party platforms like Zapier, Make (formerly Integromat), and Workato allow you to create complex workflows between Airtable and thousands of other apps.

- **Example**: Use Zapier to add new Airtable records to a Google Sheet.

3. API Integrations

Airtable's robust API allows developers to build custom integrations tailored to specific needs.

- **Example**: Sync Airtable data with a custom-built CRM or analytics dashboard.

4. Webhooks

Webhooks enable Airtable to communicate with other services in real time, triggering events based on changes in your Airtable base.

- **Example**: Trigger a webhook to update a Shopify inventory when a new order is added to Airtable.

Common Third-Party Integrations

1. Email Marketing

- **Tools**: Mailchimp, ActiveCampaign, SendGrid
- **Use Case**: Automatically add new Airtable contacts to an email list and send personalized campaigns.
- **Example Workflow**:
    1. Trigger: When a new record is added to a "Leads" table.
    2. Action: Add the contact to a Mailchimp list and send a welcome email.

2. Project Management

- **Tools**: Trello, Asana, ClickUp
- **Use Case**: Convert Airtable records into tasks or cards in project management tools.
- **Example Workflow**:
    1. Trigger: When a record is created in a "Tasks" table.
    2. Action: Create a new Trello card with task details.

3. Customer Relationship Management (CRM)

- **Tools**: Salesforce, HubSpot, Zoho CRM
- **Use Case**: Sync Airtable records with your CRM to manage leads and track customer interactions.
- **Example Workflow**:
    1. Trigger: When a lead's status changes to "Qualified" in Airtable.
    2. Action: Add the lead to Salesforce and assign it to a sales rep.

4. Communication and Collaboration

- **Tools**: Slack, Microsoft Teams, Zoom
- **Use Case**: Notify team members of updates or changes in Airtable.
- **Example Workflow**:
    1. Trigger: When a record in the "Projects" table is marked as "Complete."
    2. Action: Send a Slack message to the project team.

5. Analytics and Reporting

- **Tools**: Google Sheets, Google Data Studio, Tableau
- **Use Case**: Export Airtable data for advanced reporting and visualization.
- **Example Workflow**:
    1. Trigger: When a record is added or updated in Airtable.
    2. Action: Sync the data to Google Sheets for detailed analysis.

6. E-Commerce

- **Tools**: Shopify, WooCommerce, Stripe
- **Use Case**: Manage inventory, track orders, or sync payments with Airtable.
- **Example Workflow**:
    1. Trigger: When a new order is placed in Shopify.
    2. Action: Add the order to Airtable and update inventory levels.

Setting Up an Integration with Zapier

Zapier is a user-friendly platform that connects Airtable to thousands of other apps. Follow these steps to set up an integration:

Step 1: Create a Zapier Account

1. Sign up for a free Zapier account at zapier.com.
2. Log in and click **"Create Zap"** to start building your workflow.

Step 2: Choose a Trigger

1. Select **Airtable** as the trigger app.
2. Choose a trigger event, such as "New Record in View."
3. Connect your Airtable account and select the base and table to monitor.

Step 3: Choose an Action

1. Select the app you want to connect with Airtable (e.g., Gmail, Slack, or Trello).
2. Choose an action event, such as "Send Email" or "Create Task."
3. Map the fields from Airtable to the fields in the action app (e.g., map the "Email" field in Airtable to the "To" field in Gmail).

Step 4: Test the Integration

1. Run a test to ensure the integration works as expected.
2. Check that the action app received the data correctly.

Step 5: Turn On the Zap

Once tested, turn on the Zap to activate the integration.

Best Practices for Third-Party Integrations

1. Start Small

Begin with simple workflows to get comfortable with the integration process. Gradually add complexity as needed.

2. Test Thoroughly

Test integrations before deploying them to ensure they function as intended and handle edge cases.

3. Monitor and Optimize

Regularly review your integrations to ensure they're running efficiently. Address any errors or performance issues promptly.

4. Use Secure Connections

Ensure all integrations use secure connections (e.g., HTTPS) and follow data security best practices.

5. Document Workflows

Keep a record of your integrations, including trigger and action details, to make troubleshooting and scaling easier.

Challenges and Solutions

Challenge 1: Data Mismatches

- **Problem**: Fields in Airtable and the third-party tool don't align.
- **Solution**: Use formula fields in Airtable to format data appropriately before syncing.

Challenge 2: Integration Errors

- **Problem**: Automations fail due to changes in Airtable or the connected app.
- **Solution**: Regularly test and update your integrations to reflect changes in your workflows.

Challenge 3: Run Limits

- **Problem**: Platforms like Zapier have usage limits on free plans.
- **Solution**: Upgrade to a paid plan or explore alternatives like Make.

Conclusion

Integrating Airtable with third-party services unlocks endless possibilities for automating workflows and enhancing productivity. By leveraging tools like Zapier, Make, and Airtable's API, you can create powerful connections that simplify your processes and centralize your data.

Optimizing Automated Workflows

While setting up automations in Airtable can save time and reduce manual effort, optimizing those workflows ensures they run efficiently, scale effectively, and meet your growing needs. Poorly designed automations can lead to unnecessary resource consumption, errors, or delays. This chapter focuses on strategies, tools, and best practices to optimize your automated workflows, ensuring they remain efficient, reliable, and aligned with your goals.

Why Optimize Automated Workflows?

Optimizing workflows enhances productivity by:

- **Reducing Redundancy**: Eliminating repetitive or overlapping automations.
- **Improving Speed**: Ensuring workflows run quickly and without delays.
- **Minimizing Errors**: Preventing conflicts or unintended actions.
- **Scaling Seamlessly**: Adapting workflows to handle increased volume or complexity.

Key Principles of Workflow Optimization

1. Keep Automations Focused

- Design automations to perform specific tasks rather than attempting to handle multiple processes within a single workflow.
- Use separate automations for unrelated tasks to maintain clarity and prevent conflicts.

2. Minimize Trigger Frequency

- Avoid automations that run too frequently or monitor too many records.
- Use filters or conditions to limit triggers to relevant records.
  - **Example**: Instead of triggering an automation for every record update, configure it to activate only when a specific field (e.g., "Status") changes.

3. Test Before Deployment

- Run tests for new or updated automations to ensure they work as intended.
- Verify that automations handle edge cases and unexpected inputs correctly.

4. Monitor Automation Performance

- Regularly review automation logs to identify issues, such as errors or excessive runs.
- Adjust workflows based on log insights to improve efficiency.

Techniques for Optimizing Workflow Components

1. Optimize Triggers

Triggers determine when automations run, so optimizing them can significantly impact performance:

- **Use Conditional Triggers**: Set conditions to ensure automations only activate when necessary.
- **Avoid Broad Triggers**: Limit triggers to specific tables, views, or fields to reduce unnecessary runs.

2. Streamline Actions

Actions define what automations do, and optimizing them can save time and resources:

- **Batch Updates**: Combine related updates into a single action where possible.
- **Avoid Complex Chains**: Limit the number of sequential actions to reduce processing time.
- **Use Defaults**: Set default values in fields to simplify action configuration.

3. Use Scheduled Automations Wisely

Scheduled automations can be resource-intensive if overused:

- **Combine Scheduled Tasks**: Consolidate similar tasks into a single automation that runs at a specific time.
- **Adjust Frequency**: Use the minimum frequency required (e.g., daily instead of hourly).

Advanced Optimization Strategies

1. Implement Dependency Tracking

For complex workflows, track dependencies to ensure automations run in the correct order.

- Use a **status field** or **timestamp field** to signal when a record is ready for the next automation.
- Example: An automation that updates a task's status triggers a second automation to notify the assigned team member.

2. Use Linked Records for Data Relationships

Instead of duplicating data across tables, use linked records to reference related information.

- Example: Instead of copying customer details into every order record, link orders to a "Customers" table and use lookup fields.

3. Leverage Formula Fields

Use formula fields to calculate or transform data before automations run, reducing the need for complex actions.

- Example: Use a formula to calculate "Days Until Due Date" and trigger an automation only when the value is less than 3.

4. Integrate with External Tools

For advanced workflows, consider integrating Airtable with external tools like Zapier, Make, or custom scripts. These platforms can handle more complex logic or multi-step workflows.

- Example: Use Zapier to create a multi-step process that involves Airtable, Slack, and Google Sheets.

Common Workflow Challenges and Solutions

Challenge 1: Automation Errors

- **Cause**: Misconfigured triggers or actions.

- **Solution**: Double-check field mappings, test automations thoroughly, and review logs to identify and fix issues.

Challenge 2: Workflow Overlap

- **Cause**: Multiple automations triggered by the same event.
- **Solution**: Consolidate overlapping workflows into a single automation or use distinct triggers for each.

Challenge 3: Delayed Execution

- **Cause**: High automation frequency or complex actions.
- **Solution**: Limit trigger frequency, simplify actions, and batch updates where possible.

Challenge 4: Scaling Issues

- **Cause**: Workflows fail to handle increased data volume or complexity.
- **Solution**: Optimize triggers, actions, and dependencies to ensure scalability.

Tools for Monitoring and Optimizing Workflows

1. Airtable Logs

- View automation logs to track activity, identify errors, and monitor performance.

2. External Monitoring Tools

- Use tools like Make or Zapier to visualize and manage multi-platform workflows.

3. Airtable Scripting Block

- For advanced users, use scripting blocks to create custom scripts that optimize or enhance workflow components.

Best Practices for Workflow Optimization

1. **Start Simple**: Build and test basic workflows before adding complexity.
2. **Document Workflows**: Keep a record of automation purposes, triggers, and actions for easier troubleshooting.
3. **Regularly Review Workflows**: Periodically audit automations to ensure they remain relevant and efficient.
4. **Train Your Team**: Ensure all collaborators understand how workflows operate and their impact on the base.
5. **Monitor Usage Limits**: Be aware of Airtable's automation and run limits, especially on free or lower-tier plans.

Real-World Examples

1. Task Notifications

- **Optimized Workflow**: Notify team members only when high-priority tasks are assigned to them, instead of sending notifications for all tasks.

- **Implementation**: Use a conditional trigger to filter tasks by priority.

2. Weekly Reports

- **Optimized Workflow**: Generate a summary of new leads weekly instead of sending real-time updates for each lead.
- **Implementation**: Use a scheduled automation to compile and send reports every Monday morning.

3. Customer Feedback Processing

- **Optimized Workflow**: Automatically categorize and prioritize feedback based on sentiment.
- **Implementation**: Use a formula field to analyze sentiment and trigger actions for high-priority feedback only.

Conclusion

Optimizing automated workflows in Airtable ensures your processes run smoothly, efficiently, and without unnecessary complexity. By following the strategies and best practices outlined in this chapter, you can reduce errors, improve scalability, and maximize the value of your automations.

Section 7:
Building Interfaces and Web Apps

Introduction to Interfaces

Interfaces in Airtable are a game-changing feature that allows you to create user-friendly, visually engaging dashboards tailored to your team's needs. With interfaces, you can transform raw data into intuitive views, making it easier to analyze, share, and act on information. Whether you're tracking project progress, managing customer relationships, or building a reporting dashboard, interfaces let you present your data in a way that is both functional and aesthetically pleasing.

This chapter introduces Airtable interfaces, explores their benefits, and provides a roadmap for getting started with building your first interface.

What Are Airtable Interfaces?

Airtable interfaces are custom, interactive dashboards built on top of your Airtable base. They allow you to:

- **Visualize Data**: Present data in charts, grids, and forms for better decision-making.
- **Simplify Interaction**: Provide a streamlined view of data, showing only the most relevant fields and records.
- **Enhance Collaboration**: Create interfaces tailored to specific team members or roles.
- **Increase Accessibility**: Make Airtable easier to use for non-technical users by reducing complexity.

Benefits of Using Interfaces

1. Customization

Design interfaces that match your team's workflow by including only the data and tools they need.

2. Better Data Insights

Visual components like charts and summaries make it easier to identify trends, track progress, and make informed decisions.

3. Improved Usability

Interfaces simplify complex databases, allowing users to interact with data without navigating tables, filters, or views.

4. Tailored Access

Create different interfaces for different users or teams, showing only the data relevant to their role.

5. No-Code Simplicity

Building interfaces requires no coding knowledge, making it accessible to anyone familiar with Airtable.

Key Features of Airtable Interfaces

1. Widgets

Widgets are the building blocks of interfaces, allowing you to display data in various formats:

- **Record Lists**: Display a list of records that users can filter or sort.
- **Charts**: Visualize data trends with bar charts, line charts, or pie charts.
- **Summary Blocks**: Show aggregated data like totals or averages.
- **Forms**: Allow users to add or edit records directly from the interface.

2. Interactivity

Interfaces allow users to:

- Apply filters to focus on specific data.
- Click on records to view detailed information.
- Update data directly from the interface without switching to the base.

3. Real-Time Updates

Changes made in the interface reflect instantly in the underlying base, ensuring everyone is always working with the latest data.

4. Role-Based Views

Design interfaces for specific use cases, such as team dashboards, project trackers, or sales pipelines, and share them with the relevant users.

Getting Started with Interfaces

Step 1: Open the Interface Designer

1. Open the Airtable base you want to use for your interface.
2. Click the **"Interfaces"** tab at the top of the screen.
3. Select **"Create a new interface"** to begin.

Step 2: Choose a Layout

Airtable offers pre-built templates to help you get started quickly:

- **Dashboard**: Ideal for tracking metrics and visualizing key data points.
- **Record Review**: Focused on viewing and managing individual records.
- **Form-Focused**: Great for creating input forms or simple data-entry interfaces.

Alternatively, you can start with a blank layout for complete customization.

Step 3: Add Widgets

1. Drag and drop widgets onto the interface canvas.
2. Configure each widget to display data from your base. For example:
   - Use a **Record List** widget to show all open tasks.
   - Add a **Bar Chart** widget to display the number of tasks by priority.

   ○ Include a **Form** widget to allow users to submit new tasks.

Step 4: Customize the Design

1. Adjust the layout, colors, and fonts to match your branding.
2. Use headers and text blocks to provide context or instructions.

Step 5: Share the Interface

1. Click **"Share"** to make the interface accessible to others.
2. Define permissions to control who can view or edit the interface.

Example Use Cases for Interfaces

1. Project Management Dashboard

- **Widgets**: Task list, progress chart, and summary of completed tasks.
- **Use Case**: Provide a real-time overview of project progress for team members.

2. Sales Pipeline Tracker

- **Widgets**: Record list of leads, chart of deals by stage, and summary of total revenue.
- **Use Case**: Help sales teams track leads and monitor deal progress.

3. Content Calendar

- **Widgets**: Calendar view of publishing dates, list of upcoming tasks, and a form for new content ideas.
- **Use Case**: Streamline editorial planning and ensure deadlines are met.

4. Customer Feedback Hub

- **Widgets**: List of feedback entries, sentiment analysis chart, and a form for submitting feedback.
- **Use Case**: Centralize customer feedback and track common themes or issues.

Best Practices for Designing Interfaces

1. Keep It Simple

- Focus on the most relevant data and avoid cluttering the interface with unnecessary details.

2. Use Filters Effectively

- Allow users to filter records by fields like status, date, or priority for a more focused view.

3. Test with End Users

- Share the interface with a small group of users for feedback and iterate based on their suggestions.

4. Maintain Consistency

- Use consistent colors, fonts, and layout styles across all interfaces for a cohesive user experience.

5. Update Regularly

- Keep interfaces up to date as your workflows or data change.

Troubleshooting Common Issues

1. Missing Data in Widgets

- **Cause**: The widget is not connected to the correct table or view.
- **Solution**: Double-check the data source and reconfigure the widget.

2. Slow Loading Times

- **Cause**: The interface includes too many complex widgets.
- **Solution**: Simplify the interface by reducing the number of widgets or limiting the data shown.

3. Permissions Issues

- **Cause**: Users don't have the necessary permissions to access the interface.
- **Solution**: Adjust sharing settings to grant appropriate access.

Conclusion

Interfaces transform Airtable into a dynamic tool that is not only powerful but also accessible to a wider audience. By designing tailored dashboards and workflows, you can enhance collaboration, simplify complex data, and empower your team to make data-driven decisions.

Creating a Simple Interface for Your Base

Creating a simple interface for your Airtable base transforms how users interact with your data. Instead of navigating tables and views, an interface provides a clear, user-friendly way to view, update, and manage records. This is especially useful for teams with varying levels of technical expertise, as it simplifies the data management process while maintaining functionality and interactivity.

In this chapter, you'll learn how to create a simple interface step by step, understand the components of an interface, and discover how to make it both practical and visually appealing.

Why Build a Simple Interface?

A well-designed interface can:

- **Simplify Complex Data**: Present only the most relevant information to users.
- **Streamline Workflow**: Provide quick access to frequently used tools and views.
- **Improve Collaboration**: Allow team members to interact with data in a focused, intuitive way.
- **Enhance Usability**: Reduce the learning curve for non-technical users.

Steps to Create a Simple Interface

Step 1: Open the Interface Designer

1. Open the Airtable base you want to use.
2. Click the **"Interfaces"** tab at the top of the Airtable workspace.
3. Click **"Create a new interface"** to start building your interface.

Step 2: Choose a Template or Start from Scratch

- Airtable offers several templates to get you started:
  - **Record Review**: Focuses on viewing and editing individual records.
  - **Dashboard**: Ideal for presenting summaries and key metrics.
  - **Form-Focused**: Simplifies data entry.
- For full control, choose the **Blank Layout** option to create your own design.

Step 3: Select a Data Source

1. Choose the table and view you want the interface to connect to.
2. This ensures the interface reflects the data structure and filters of your chosen view.

Step 4: Add Widgets to the Interface

Widgets are the building blocks of your interface. Drag and drop widgets onto the canvas to customize the interface layout.

Common Widgets:

1. **Record List**: Displays a list of records from your table.
   - Example: Show a list of ongoing projects or tasks.
2. **Record Details**: Displays detailed information about a selected record.
   - Example: View all fields for a specific customer.
3. **Chart**: Visualizes data trends.
   - Example: Show the distribution of tasks by status using a bar chart.

4. **Button**: Adds interactivity by triggering actions like opening a form or updating a record.
   - Example: Add a "Mark as Complete" button for tasks.
5. **Form**: Allows users to submit or update data directly from the interface.
   - Example: Add a form for creating new leads or logging feedback.

Step 5: Customize the Layout

1. Resize and position widgets to create a clean, organized layout.
2. Use text blocks or headers to provide context, such as titles or instructions.
3. Group related widgets together to enhance usability.

Step 6: Configure Widget Settings

1. Click on each widget to adjust its settings.
   - Example: For a record list, specify which fields to display or filter records by specific criteria.
2. Use filters to show only relevant data, such as tasks assigned to the logged-in user.
3. Enable interactivity, such as allowing users to update records directly from the interface.

Step 7: Preview and Test

1. Click the **"Preview"** button to see how the interface looks and functions.
2. Test each widget to ensure it works as intended.
3. Make adjustments based on your testing to improve usability and design.

Step 8: Share the Interface

1. Click the **"Share"** button to make the interface accessible to others.
2. Define permissions for users:
   - **View Only**: Users can view data but cannot make changes.
   - **Full Access**: Users can interact with widgets and update records.

Example: Building a Task Management Interface

Let's create a simple interface for managing tasks in a "Tasks" table.

1. **Data Source**: Connect the interface to the "Tasks" table.
2. **Widgets**:
   - Add a **Record List** to show all tasks.
   - Add a **Record Details** widget to display details for a selected task.
   - Add a **Button** widget labeled "Mark as Complete" to update the task status.
3. **Filters**: Configure the record list to show only tasks where "Status" is not "Completed."
4. **Layout**: Position the widgets side by side for a clean and efficient design.
5. **Testing**: Preview the interface and test the button to ensure it updates the task status correctly.

Best Practices for Simple Interfaces

1. Focus on the User

- Design interfaces with the end user in mind.
- Include only the most relevant data and widgets to avoid overwhelming users.

2. Use Clear Labels

- Label widgets and buttons clearly to guide users.

- Add instructions or tooltips for complex workflows.

3. Maintain Consistency

- Use consistent colors, fonts, and spacing for a professional look.
- Align widgets to create a clean, organized layout.

4. Test Before Sharing

- Test the interface with real users to identify usability issues and make improvements.

5. Update Regularly

- Keep interfaces up to date as your workflows or data evolve.

Troubleshooting Common Issues

1. Widgets Not Displaying Data

- **Cause**: The widget is not connected to the correct table or view.
- **Solution**: Reconfigure the widget's data source.

2. Interface Layout Looks Cluttered

- **Cause**: Too many widgets or poorly organized components.
- **Solution**: Simplify the layout and group related widgets together.

3. Permissions Errors

- **Cause**: Users lack the necessary access to the interface or base.
- **Solution**: Adjust sharing settings and permissions.

Conclusion

Building a simple interface in Airtable enables you to create tailored, user-friendly dashboards that enhance collaboration and productivity. By following the steps and best practices outlined in this chapter, you can design an interface that simplifies data management and empowers your team.

Publishing Your Interface as a Web App

One of the standout features of Airtable is its ability to create and share interfaces as web apps. Publishing your interface as a web app allows your team, clients, or stakeholders to interact with your data in a streamlined, user-friendly environment without requiring access to the Airtable base itself. This functionality is perfect for creating dashboards, portals, or custom workflows tailored to specific audiences.

In this chapter, we'll explore how to publish your Airtable interface as a web app, configure access settings, and ensure a seamless user experience.

What Does It Mean to Publish an Interface as a Web App?

Publishing an interface as a web app means making it accessible via a public or private URL. Users who visit the URL can interact with the interface, view data, and perform actions based on the permissions you set. This is particularly useful for:

- Sharing dashboards with external stakeholders.
- Allowing clients to submit or update information.
- Creating standalone portals for internal or external use.

Benefits of Publishing Interfaces as Web Apps

1. Accessibility

Provide users with access to the interface without requiring them to log into Airtable or navigate complex data tables.

2. Customization

Design the interface to show only the data and tools relevant to your audience, improving usability.

3. Real-Time Updates

Changes made in Airtable are reflected in the web app immediately, ensuring users always see the latest data.

4. Increased Collaboration

Enable users to view, update, or submit data directly through the web app, streamlining workflows.

5. Professional Presentation

A well-designed web app adds a layer of professionalism, especially when shared with clients or external stakeholders.

Steps to Publish Your Interface as a Web App

Step 1: Finalize Your Interface Design

Before publishing, ensure your interface is complete and functional:

1. Test all widgets to confirm they display data correctly and respond to user interactions.

2. Review the layout for clarity and usability.
3. Add headers, labels, or instructions to guide users.

Step 2: Open the Share Settings

1. In the Airtable interface builder, click the **"Share"** button in the top-right corner.
2. This will open the sharing options for your interface.

Step 3: Choose the Sharing Method

Airtable offers two primary ways to share your interface:

1. **Invite Users**: Share the interface with specific individuals by entering their email addresses.
   ○ Best for internal teams or restricted access.
2. **Generate a Shareable Link**: Create a public or private link that can be shared with a broader audience.
   ○ Best for external stakeholders or clients.

Step 4: Configure Permissions

1. Select the level of access users will have:
   ○ **Viewer**: Users can view data but cannot make changes.
   ○ **Editor**: Users can interact with the interface and update data.
2. For public links, decide whether users need to log in with an Airtable account or can access the interface anonymously.

Step 5: Copy and Share the Link

1. Once configured, copy the link and share it via email, chat, or other communication channels.
2. Test the link yourself to ensure the interface appears and functions as intended.

Customizing the Web App Experience

1. Add Branding Elements

Make your web app visually appealing and professional by including:

- Your organization's logo.
- Custom headers or footers with branding.
- A consistent color scheme.

2. Optimize for Different Devices

Ensure your interface is responsive and works well on both desktop and mobile devices:

- Test the interface on multiple screen sizes.
- Use widgets that scale gracefully, such as charts and record lists.

3. Provide Clear Instructions

Include a brief guide or text block to explain how users can interact with the web app. For example:

- Where to find key information.
- How to submit or update data.

4. Use Filters for Personalized Views

If sharing the web app with multiple users, apply filters to show only the data relevant to each user. For example:

- Display only the tasks assigned to the logged-in user.
- Show data based on specific categories or locations.

Example Use Cases

1. Client Portals

- Use Case: Share project progress with clients.
- Features:
    - A dashboard summarizing key metrics.
    - A record list showing completed and pending tasks.
    - A form for clients to submit requests or feedback.

2. Event Management

- Use Case: Allow attendees to RSVP and view event details.
- Features:
    - A calendar widget showing event dates.
    - A form for RSVPs.
    - A summary block displaying the total number of attendees.

3. Sales Dashboards

- Use Case: Share real-time sales data with the team.
- Features:
    - Charts showing sales by region or product.
    - A record list of leads and opportunities.
    - Filters to view data for specific sales reps.

Best Practices for Publishing Interfaces

1. Secure Sensitive Data

- Use filters and permissions to ensure users only see data they are authorized to access.
- Avoid sharing private or confidential information in public links.

2. Test Before Launch

- Test the web app as if you were an end user to identify any usability issues.
- Verify that all links, buttons, and forms work correctly.

3. Monitor Usage

- Periodically review how the web app is being used.
- Collect feedback from users to make improvements.

4. Update Regularly

- Keep the interface up to date as your data or workflows evolve.
- Add new features or widgets to enhance the user experience.

Troubleshooting Common Issues

1. Users Can't Access the Web App

- **Cause**: Incorrect sharing settings or permissions.
- **Solution**: Ensure the link is active and permissions are set correctly.

2. Data Isn't Updating in Real-Time

- **Cause**: Issues with syncing between the base and the interface.
- **Solution**: Refresh the interface and check for errors in the base.

3. Interface Layout Looks Broken on Mobile

- **Cause**: Widgets are not optimized for smaller screens.
- **Solution**: Adjust widget sizes and test the layout on mobile devices.

Conclusion

Publishing your Airtable interface as a web app provides a powerful way to share data and workflows with your team or external stakeholders. By customizing the interface, configuring permissions, and following best practices, you can create a seamless, professional experience for your users.

Styling and Customization Options

Styling and customizing your Airtable interface is essential for creating a polished, professional, and user-friendly experience. Whether you're building an internal dashboard for your team or a client-facing web app, customization ensures the interface aligns with your branding, communicates information clearly, and enhances usability. In this chapter, we'll explore the various styling and customization options available in Airtable interfaces, from layout adjustments to branding elements. By the end, you'll have the tools to create interfaces that are not only functional but visually appealing.

Why Customize Your Interface?

Customizing your interface offers several benefits:

- **Improved Usability**: A clean, intuitive design makes it easier for users to interact with data.
- **Brand Consistency**: Adding your branding elements (colors, logos, fonts) creates a cohesive experience for your team or clients.
- **Enhanced Communication**: Thoughtful styling and layout help highlight key information and guide users effectively.

Key Styling Options in Airtable Interfaces

1. Layout Design

The layout is the foundation of your interface. Organizing widgets and elements properly ensures a clean, navigable design.

Best Practices for Layout Design

- **Use White Space**: Provide enough space between widgets to avoid a cluttered appearance.
- **Align Widgets**: Use Airtable's alignment tools to keep widgets neatly arranged.
- **Group Related Items**: Place widgets with similar functions or data close together.

2. Colors and Themes

Colors play a crucial role in making your interface visually appealing and on-brand.

Customizing Colors

- **Background Colors**: Choose a background color that complements your branding and ensures text and data are easy to read.
- **Widget Colors**: Some widgets, like charts, allow you to customize colors for specific data points.
- **Highlighting**: Use color coding to emphasize important data or differentiate categories.

3. Fonts and Text

Readable and consistent fonts improve the overall aesthetic of your interface.

Options for Customizing Text

- **Font Styles**: Choose from available font options to match your branding.
- **Text Sizes**: Adjust text size to ensure readability across devices.
- **Formatting**: Use bold, italic, or underlined text for emphasis.

4. Headers and Sections

Headers and sections help organize the interface into logical parts, improving navigation and usability.

How to Use Headers Effectively

- Add clear, descriptive headers to introduce each section of your interface.
- Use larger text or bold formatting for headers to make them stand out.
- Include subheadings to break down complex sections further.

5. Widgets Customization

Widgets are the primary building blocks of your interface. Customizing their appearance and behavior ensures they fit seamlessly into your design.

Customizing Widget Settings

- Adjust sizes and positions to maintain a clean layout.
- Configure filters and conditions to display only relevant data.
- For charts, choose chart types and customize colors to match your theme.

Advanced Customization Options

1. Adding Branding Elements

Incorporate your organization's branding for a professional touch:

- **Logos**: Add your company logo as an image widget at the top of the interface.
- **Colors**: Match the interface's color scheme to your brand's primary and secondary colors.

2. Conditional Visibility

Show or hide widgets based on specific conditions to create dynamic interfaces:

- **Example**: Display a "Completed Tasks" summary only when there are completed tasks.

3. Interactive Widgets

Enhance user engagement with interactive widgets like buttons and forms:

- **Buttons**: Use custom labels and colors to make actions clear and visually distinct.
- **Forms**: Customize field arrangements and placeholder text to guide users effectively.

4. Responsive Design

Ensure your interface looks great on all devices by testing and optimizing for different screen sizes:

- Use flexible layouts that adapt to smaller screens.
- Prioritize key widgets for visibility on mobile devices.

Example: Customizing a Project Dashboard Interface

Scenario

You're designing a project management dashboard for your team.

Steps to Customize

1. **Background and Theme**
   - ○ Set the background color to a light gray to reduce eye strain.
   - ○ Use your company's primary color for header text and chart accents.
2. **Header and Sections**
   - ○ Add a bold header at the top: "Team Project Dashboard."
   - ○ Create sections for "Ongoing Projects," "Upcoming Deadlines," and "Team Performance."
3. **Widgets Customization**
   - ○ **Record List**: Filter tasks by "Status = Ongoing" and highlight high-priority tasks with color coding.
   - ○ **Chart**: Use a bar chart to display task distribution by team member, with each member assigned a unique color.
4. **Interactive Features**
   - ○ Add a button labeled "Add New Task" that opens a pre-configured form.
   - ○ Include a summary widget showing the total number of overdue tasks.

Tips for Effective Customization

1. **Keep It Simple**: Avoid overloading the interface with too many widgets or design elements.
2. **Be Consistent**: Use a consistent color scheme and font style throughout the interface.
3. **Focus on Key Data**: Highlight the most important information to guide users' attention.
4. **Test on Real Users**: Gather feedback from your team or clients to ensure the design meets their needs.
5. **Iterate and Improve**: Regularly update the interface as workflows or requirements change.

Common Pitfalls to Avoid

1. Overcrowded Layouts

- **Issue**: Too many widgets or sections make the interface hard to navigate.
- **Solution**: Prioritize essential widgets and use white space effectively.

2. Poor Color Choices

- **Issue**: Colors that are too bright or don't contrast well can strain the eyes.
- **Solution**: Use a balanced, accessible color palette.

3. Inconsistent Branding

- **Issue**: Mismatched fonts, colors, or styles create a disjointed experience.
- **Solution**: Align the design with your brand guidelines.

4. Lack of User Guidance

- **Issue**: Users don't know how to navigate or interact with the interface.
- **Solution**: Add instructions, tooltips, or a help section.

Conclusion: Styling and customization options in Airtable interfaces give you the flexibility to create professional, user-friendly designs that match your branding and improve usability. By carefully customizing layout, colors, widgets, and interactivity, you can ensure your interface meets the needs of your team or clients.

Section 8:
Beyond the Basics

Scripting with Airtable

While Airtable's no-code tools provide a powerful way to manage data and workflows, scripting takes your capabilities to the next level. By using Airtable's scripting feature, you can automate complex tasks, create custom workflows, and unlock functionality that isn't available out of the box. This chapter will introduce you to Airtable scripting, explain its benefits, and provide examples of how you can use it to supercharge your Airtable bases.

What Is Airtable Scripting?

Airtable Scripting allows users to write JavaScript code to perform custom operations directly within their Airtable base. The scripting block (found in the Airtable Marketplace) provides a coding environment where you can:

- Automate repetitive tasks.
- Transform or manipulate data.
- Integrate with external APIs.
- Create highly customized workflows.

Benefits of Scripting in Airtable

1. Enhanced Automation

Scripts allow you to automate complex workflows that go beyond Airtable's built-in automations.

2. Improved Efficiency

Save time by replacing manual data processing tasks with scripts that can execute in seconds.

3. Customization

Tailor your Airtable base to fit unique business needs by creating functionality that doesn't exist natively.

4. External Integrations

Use scripts to connect Airtable with external tools and services via APIs, such as retrieving data from third-party platforms.

Getting Started with Airtable Scripting

Step 1: Enable the Scripting Block

1. Open your Airtable base.

2. Click the **"Apps"** button in the top-right corner.
3. Select **"Add an app"** and search for the Scripting app in the Airtable Marketplace.
4. Install the app and open the scripting editor.

Step 2: Familiarize Yourself with the Environment

The scripting editor includes:

- **Code Editor**: A space to write your JavaScript code.
- **Output Panel**: Displays the results of your script or any error messages.

Step 3: Learn the Basics of Airtable's API

Airtable provides an API that allows scripts to interact with your base. Common functions include:

- **Fetching Records**: Retrieve data from a table or view.
- **Creating Records**: Add new records to a table.
- **Updating Records**: Modify existing records.
- **Deleting Records**: Remove records from a table.

Basic Scripting Examples

Example 1: Generating Reports

Generate a summary report of completed tasks and output it in the console.

```
let table = base.getTable("Tasks");
let view = table.getView("Completed Tasks");
let query = await view.selectRecordsAsync();

let completedTasks = query.records.map(record => record.getCellValue("Task Name"));

console.log("Completed Tasks:");
console.log(completedTasks.join("\n"));
```

Example 2: Bulk Update Records

Update the "Status" field of all records in a view to "Completed."

```
let table = base.getTable("Tasks");
let view = table.getView("In Progress");
let query = await view.selectRecordsAsync();

for (let record of query.records) {
    await table.updateRecordAsync(record.id, {
        "Status": "Completed"
    });
}
console.log("All tasks marked as completed.");
```

Example 3: Sending Notifications via Email

Integrate with an external email API (like SendGrid) to notify team members of overdue tasks.

```
let table = base.getTable("Tasks");
let view = table.getView("Overdue");
let query = await view.selectRecordsAsync();

let overdueTasks = query.records.map(record => record.getCellValue("Task Name"));

let emailBody = `The following tasks are overdue:\n\n${overdueTasks.join("\n")}`;

// Example integration with SendGrid API
await fetch("https://api.sendgrid.com/v3/mail/send", {
    method: "POST",
    headers: {
        "Authorization": "Bearer YOUR_SENDGRID_API_KEY",
        "Content-Type": "application/json"
    },
    body: JSON.stringify({
        personalizations: [{
            to: [{ email: "team@example.com" }]
        }],
        from: { email: "no-reply@example.com" },
        subject: "Overdue Tasks Alert",
        content: [{ type: "text/plain", value: emailBody }]
    })
});
console.log("Email notification sent.");
```

Advanced Use Cases

1. Data Cleaning and Transformation

Automatically format text fields, remove duplicates, or standardize dates across a table.

2. External Data Integration

Retrieve and update records using external APIs, such as pulling weather data or syncing with a CRM.

3. Complex Workflows

Create multi-step workflows involving multiple tables and views, such as generating invoices or assigning tasks to team members based on availability.

Best Practices for Scripting in Airtable

1. Start Simple

Begin with small, focused scripts to build your confidence and understanding of Airtable's scripting API.

2. Test Thoroughly

Test scripts on a subset of data before applying them to your entire base to avoid unintended changes.

3. Use Comments

Add comments to your code to explain what each section does. This is especially helpful for future reference or when sharing scripts with teammates.

4. Handle Errors Gracefully

Use try-catch blocks to handle potential errors and provide meaningful feedback.

```
try {
    // Your script logic here
} catch (error) {
    console.error("An error occurred:", error);
}
```

5. Keep Performance in Mind

Scripts that process large datasets can be slow. Optimize your code by filtering data early and minimizing repetitive operations.

Troubleshooting Common Issues

1. Script Won't Run

- **Cause**: Syntax errors or misconfigured API calls.
- **Solution**: Check the console for error messages and debug your code step by step.

2. Performance Issues

- **Cause**: Scripts processing too many records at once.
- **Solution**: Use filters to limit the records your script processes.

3. API Rate Limits

- **Cause**: Making too many API calls in a short time.
- **Solution**: Optimize your script and avoid unnecessary API calls.

Conclusion

Scripting in Airtable provides endless possibilities for customizing your workflows, automating tasks, and integrating with external systems. While it requires some knowledge of JavaScript, the time invested in learning scripting will pay off in the form of increased efficiency and flexibility.

Using Blocks for Extended Functionality

Airtable Blocks (now referred to as "Airtable Apps") are powerful tools that extend the functionality of your Airtable base, allowing you to visualize, analyze, and interact with your data in creative ways. From dashboards to advanced reporting, apps can transform your Airtable experience by enabling you to go beyond traditional database functionality.

In this chapter, we'll explore what Airtable Blocks (Apps) are, how to install and configure them, and how they can be used to enhance your workflows. We'll also highlight some of the most useful apps and provide real-world examples of their applications.

What Are Airtable Blocks (Apps)?

Blocks are modular apps that integrate with your Airtable base to provide additional capabilities such as:

- Visualizing data with charts, graphs, and timelines.
- Automating tasks like data exports or record updates.
- Enabling external integrations with tools like Google Maps or Slack.

They are designed to be easy to use and require no coding knowledge, making them accessible to all Airtable users.

Benefits of Using Airtable Blocks

1. Enhanced Data Visualization

Blocks like the Chart App allow you to create bar charts, line graphs, and scatter plots to visualize your data clearly and effectively.

2. Workflow Automation

Automate repetitive tasks with blocks like the Batch Update App, saving time and reducing errors.

3. Collaboration Tools

Collaborate more effectively using blocks like the Approval App, where team members can approve or reject records directly within the Airtable base.

4. Integration with External Tools

Blocks such as the Google Maps App or Send SMS App let you integrate Airtable with external platforms, enhancing its functionality.

5. Custom Dashboards

Create dynamic dashboards for real-time reporting and analysis, giving your team a clear overview of key metrics and progress.

Getting Started with Blocks

Step 1: Install a Block

1. Open your Airtable base.
2. Click the **"Apps"** button in the top-right corner.
3. Select **"Add an app"** to open the Airtable Marketplace.
4. Browse or search for the block you want to install.
5. Click **"Add app"** and configure it based on your table's data.

Step 2: Configure the Block

1. After installation, open the block and connect it to the appropriate table and view in your base.
2. Customize its settings, such as fields to display or filters to apply.
3. Save your configuration for future use.

Step 3: Use the Block

Interact with the block to visualize data, trigger actions, or analyze information based on your setup.

Popular Airtable Blocks

1. Chart App

Visualize your data with charts and graphs to identify trends and insights quickly.

- **Use Case**: Create a bar chart to track project progress or a pie chart to analyze task distribution.

2. Timeline App

Visualize records with date fields on an interactive timeline.

- **Use Case**: Plan events or manage project schedules with start and end dates.

3. Batch Update App

Update multiple records at once based on specified criteria.

- **Use Case**: Change the status of all overdue tasks to "Urgent" in bulk.

4. Google Maps App

Plot address or location data on a map.

- **Use Case**: Visualize customer locations or plan delivery routes.

5. Pivot Table App

Summarize and analyze data using pivot tables for advanced reporting.

- **Use Case**: Break down sales revenue by product category or region.

6. Page Designer App

Design and print customized documents such as invoices, labels, or reports.

- **Use Case**: Generate professional invoices for clients directly from Airtable records.

7. SendGrid App

Send emails directly from your Airtable base using SendGrid.

- **Use Case**: Send automated email updates to clients or stakeholders based on record changes.

8. Dashboard Blocks

Combine multiple blocks into a single dashboard for real-time reporting and monitoring.

- **Use Case**: Create a project dashboard showing task progress, team workload, and upcoming deadlines.

Example: Using Blocks for a Sales Dashboard

Imagine you're building a sales dashboard to track key metrics.

1. **Install Relevant Blocks**
   - Chart App: Visualize sales by region.
   - Summary Block: Display total revenue and the number of closed deals.
   - Google Maps App: Plot customer locations for better geographic insights.
2. **Configure Each Block**
   - Connect the Chart App to your "Sales" table and group data by "Region."
   - Use the Summary Block to calculate the total revenue field.
   - Link the Google Maps App to the "Customer Address" field.
3. **Combine into a Dashboard**
   - Arrange all blocks into a single interface for an at-a-glance view of your sales performance.

Advanced Customization with Blocks

1. Combining Multiple Blocks

Use multiple blocks together to create interactive dashboards or workflows. For example:

- Combine the Timeline App and Chart App to track project deadlines and visualize task distribution.

2. Real-Time Updates

Most blocks update automatically as data changes in your base, ensuring you're always working with the latest information.

3. Export and Share

Export data visualizations or reports from blocks like the Page Designer App to share with clients or team members.

Best Practices for Using Blocks

1. Start with Core Blocks

Begin with blocks that align with your current workflows, such as the Chart App or Timeline App.

2. Test Before Deployment

Ensure blocks are properly configured and provide accurate results before sharing them with your team.

3. Keep It Simple

Avoid overcrowding your interface with too many blocks. Focus on the most impactful visualizations and tools.

4. Update Regularly

As your workflows or data evolve, update the blocks to reflect the latest requirements.

Troubleshooting Common Issues

1. Data Isn't Displaying Correctly

- **Cause**: The block is connected to the wrong table or view.
- **Solution**: Reconfigure the block's data source and filters.

2. Performance Issues

- **Cause**: Large datasets may slow down certain blocks.
- **Solution**: Filter data in your view to reduce the number of records processed.

3. Limited Functionality

- **Cause**: The block may not support a specific feature you need.
- **Solution**: Explore alternative blocks or consider using Airtable's scripting feature.

Conclusion

Airtable Blocks (Apps) unlock a world of possibilities for visualizing, analyzing, and interacting with your data. By integrating blocks into your workflows, you can create powerful dashboards, automate tasks, and customize Airtable to meet your unique needs.

Performance Considerations

As your Airtable base grows in complexity, with more tables, records, and collaborators, performance can become a critical factor in maintaining productivity. Slow loading times, sluggish responses, and cumbersome workflows can hinder the user experience. To ensure your base remains fast and efficient, it's important to adopt best practices and optimize your data structure, workflows, and integrations.

In this chapter, we'll explore the key factors that affect Airtable performance and provide practical tips to keep your base running smoothly, no matter its size or complexity.

Factors That Affect Airtable Performance

1. Number of Records

The more records in a table, the longer it can take for views and filters to load. Bases with tens of thousands of records can experience significant slowdowns.

2. Field Complexity

Fields like formulas, rollups, and linked records can be computationally intensive, especially when applied to large datasets.

3. Views and Filters

Complex views with multiple filters, groupings, or sorts can slow down performance, especially when used across many tables.

4. Collaborator Activity

Multiple collaborators editing or interacting with the same base simultaneously can lead to syncing delays.

5. Automations and Scripts

Frequent or inefficient automations and scripts can consume resources and impact base responsiveness.

Best Practices for Optimizing Performance

1. Optimize Your Data Structure

Use Fewer Fields

- Avoid excessive use of computed fields like formulas and rollups.
- Only include fields that are necessary for your workflows.

Split Large Tables

- If a table contains tens of thousands of records, consider splitting it into smaller, related tables using linked records.

Archive Old Records

- Move outdated or inactive records to an archive table to reduce the size of active tables.

Minimize Linked Records

- Use linked records sparingly, as they require additional processing to maintain relationships between tables.

2. Streamline Views and Filters

Reduce View Complexity

- Simplify views by limiting the number of filters, sorts, and groupings.
- Create views tailored to specific tasks or users rather than using a single, catch-all view.

Use Conditional Filters

- Apply filters that dynamically reduce the number of visible records, such as "Status is not Completed."

3. Manage Automations Efficiently

Limit Automation Frequency

- Avoid triggering automations for every record update. Use conditions to run automations only when necessary.

Optimize Automation Steps

- Consolidate steps in your automations to minimize resource usage.

Monitor Automation Performance

- Regularly review automation logs to identify and resolve slow or failing workflows.

4. Use External Tools for Heavy Lifting

For computationally intensive tasks, consider exporting data to external tools like Excel, Google Sheets, or a dedicated data processing platform. This approach can offload heavy calculations from Airtable and improve performance.

Strategies for Handling Large Datasets

1. Paginate Your Data

- Break down large datasets into smaller, manageable chunks using views or filters.

2. Use Summary Tables

- Create summary tables that aggregate data using rollups or lookups instead of directly interacting with large datasets.

3. Limit Record Updates

- Minimize the frequency of updates to large datasets by using batch processing scripts or automation triggers.

4. Enable Lazy Loading

- When working with large tables, Airtable automatically uses lazy loading to display only the data visible in the current view. Use this feature to your advantage by creating compact, focused views.

Real-World Example: Optimizing a Sales CRM Base

Scenario

A sales team is using a CRM base with 20,000 customer records, each with linked tasks, notes, and sales activities. The base is experiencing slow performance.

Optimization Steps

1. **Archive Inactive Customers**
   - Move customers who haven't interacted in over a year to an archive table.
2. **Simplify Views**
   - Create separate views for "Active Leads" and "Closed Deals" instead of displaying all records in one view.
3. **Optimize Linked Records**
   - Replace some linked records with summary fields to reduce computational overhead.
4. **Streamline Automations**
   - Modify automations to trigger only when a customer's "Status" field changes to "Qualified Lead."
5. **Use External Reporting Tools**
   - Export data to Google Sheets for complex reporting, reducing the strain on Airtable.

Troubleshooting Performance Issues

1. Slow Loading Times

- **Cause**: Too many records or complex views.
- **Solution**: Simplify views, archive old data, and limit the number of displayed records.

2. Automations Failing to Trigger

- **Cause**: Too many automation triggers or excessive resource usage.
- **Solution**: Review and optimize automation conditions and frequency.

3. Script Errors

- **Cause**: Scripts attempting to process too many records simultaneously.
- **Solution**: Add pagination or process records in batches.

4. Delayed Updates

- **Cause**: High collaborator activity or frequent record updates.
- **Solution**: Coordinate collaborator activity and reduce update frequency.

Best Practices for Scalable Bases

1. Plan for Growth

Design your base with scalability in mind, anticipating future data and workflow needs.

2. Regularly Audit Your Base

Periodically review your tables, views, fields, and automations to identify areas for improvement.

3. Train Your Team

Ensure team members understand best practices for working with large datasets, including using focused views and avoiding unnecessary updates.

4. Leverage Airtable Support

If you encounter persistent performance issues, reach out to Airtable support for guidance.

Conclusion

Performance optimization is essential for maintaining a fast and efficient Airtable base, especially as your data and workflows grow. By streamlining your data structure, simplifying views, and managing automations effectively, you can ensure your base remains responsive and user-friendly.

Troubleshooting Common Issues

Even with its intuitive design and powerful features, Airtable isn't immune to occasional challenges. Users may encounter issues ranging from automations failing to unexpected errors in data processing. This chapter focuses on common issues Airtable users face and provides practical solutions to keep your workflows running smoothly. Whether you're troubleshooting a complex automation or a simple view filter, these strategies will help you identify and resolve problems effectively.

Identifying Common Issues in Airtable

1. Performance-Related Issues

- **Slow Loading Times**: Large tables, complex views, or multiple collaborators can cause delays.
- **Lag During Updates**: Bulk updates or heavy automation usage may result in slow responses.

2. Automation Failures

- **Automations Not Triggering**: Conditions may not be met or the trigger is misconfigured.
- **Incomplete Automation Runs**: Errors occur mid-process, leaving tasks partially completed.

3. Formula Errors

- **#ERROR Displayed**: Incorrect syntax or incompatible fields can result in errors.
- **Unexpected Results**: Misconfigured formulas produce inaccurate or misleading outputs.

4. Record Linking Issues

- **Broken Linked Records**: Records fail to link correctly or links are lost.
- **Excessive Linked Records**: Too many links can lead to performance degradation.

5. Data Loss or Overwrites

- **Accidental Deletion**: Important data is deleted by a user.
- **Field Overwrites**: Fields are unintentionally overwritten during bulk updates.

6. View or Filter Problems

- **Incorrect Data Display**: Filters don't work as expected or exclude necessary records.
- **Overlapping View Configurations**: Multiple filters or groupings create confusion.

7. Collaboration Issues

- **Permission Conflicts**: Users without sufficient access rights can't view or edit data.
- **Simultaneous Edits**: Multiple users editing the same record can cause conflicts.

General Troubleshooting Steps

1. **Revisit the Basics**
   - Confirm the issue is reproducible.
   - Double-check configurations, such as view filters, formula syntax, or automation settings.
2. **Simplify the Problem**
   - Break the issue down into smaller components.
   - Test individual parts of a workflow to isolate the source of the problem.

3. **Consult Error Messages**
   - ○ Airtable often provides error messages or logs for automations, scripts, and integrations.
   - ○ Use these messages to identify and resolve the root cause.
4. **Use Version History**
   - ○ Review the revision history of a base to track changes and undo recent modifications.
5. **Ask for Help**
   - ○ Consult Airtable's support documentation or community forums for guidance.

Solutions to Specific Issues

1. Fixing Slow Loading Times

Cause: Large tables, complex views, or excessive linked records.

Solution:

- Archive old or inactive records.
- Reduce the number of filters, groupings, and sorts in views.
- Limit the use of linked records and rollups.
- Use summary tables for high-level reporting instead of working directly with large datasets.

---

2. Resolving Automation Failures

Issue: Automations aren't triggering.

Solution:

- Confirm the automation is toggled "on."
- Check the trigger conditions to ensure they are met.
- Test the trigger by manually replicating the conditions.

Issue: Automation runs but stops mid-process.

Solution:

- Review the automation log for errors.
- Simplify the automation by combining or removing unnecessary steps.
- Ensure that any referenced records or fields are present and accessible.

---

3. Debugging Formula Errors

Issue: #ERROR appears in the formula field.

Solution:

- Check for missing or mismatched parentheses.
- Ensure field names in the formula match exactly (case-sensitive).
- Verify that field types are compatible with the formula (e.g., numbers vs. text).

Issue: The formula produces unexpected results.

Solution:

- Test the formula on a smaller dataset.
- Break the formula into smaller components to isolate the issue.

- Use the "Test Formula" feature in Airtable to evaluate logic step by step.

---

4. Handling Broken Linked Records

Issue: Links are broken or fail to create.

Solution:

- Ensure that the linked table exists and is properly configured.
- Check for changes in the primary field of the linked table, as these affect link integrity.
- Avoid manual edits to linked record fields.

---

5. Preventing Data Loss

Issue: Records or fields are accidentally deleted.

Solution:

- Use the "Undo" feature immediately after deletion.
- Restore data from Airtable's revision history.
- Enable field locking for sensitive fields to prevent accidental edits.

Issue: Fields are overwritten unintentionally.

Solution:

- Use restricted permissions to limit editing access.
- Implement a secondary approval process before bulk updates.

---

6. Fixing View or Filter Problems

Issue: Filters don't display the correct records.

Solution:

- Review filter conditions to ensure they are accurate and relevant.
- Check for conflicting filters or groupings in the view.

Issue: Views are cluttered or confusing.

Solution:

- Create dedicated views for specific users or tasks.
- Add clear naming conventions to views for better organization.

---

7. Resolving Collaboration Conflicts

Issue: Users can't access or edit data.

Solution:

- Confirm user permissions match their role.
- Use shared views with limited access for external collaborators.

Issue: Simultaneous edits cause data conflicts.

Solution:

- Encourage users to work in separate views to reduce overlap.
- Regularly communicate with team members about active edits.

Tools and Resources for Troubleshooting

1. Revision History

- Use Airtable's version history to identify when changes occurred and who made them.

2. Automation Logs

- View detailed logs for each automation run to identify where errors occur.

3. Airtable Support and Community

- Access Airtable's help center, tutorials, and active community forums for additional assistance.

4. External Tools

- Use third-party tools like Zapier or Make for advanced troubleshooting and integrations.

Preventative Measures

- **Train Your Team**: Provide team members with best practices to avoid common issues.
- **Regular Audits**: Periodically review your base's structure, automations, and permissions.
- **Backup Data**: Export data regularly to ensure you have a copy in case of accidental loss.

Conclusion

Troubleshooting issues in Airtable doesn't have to be daunting. By systematically identifying the root cause, leveraging Airtable's built-in tools, and following best practices, you can resolve most problems efficiently. The key is to remain proactive—plan your workflows carefully, monitor performance, and train your team to minimize errors.

Section 9:
Practical Use Cases

Project Management and Task Tracking

Airtable is a versatile tool for managing projects and tracking tasks, combining the flexibility of a spreadsheet with the power of a database. Its customizable views, collaboration features, and automations make it an ideal platform for project management. Whether you're managing a small team or a complex project with multiple stakeholders, Airtable can help you stay organized, track progress, and ensure timely delivery.

In this chapter, we'll explore how to set up an effective project management and task tracking system in Airtable. From creating task lists to automating notifications, you'll learn how to optimize your workflows and boost team productivity.

Setting Up Your Project Management Base

Step 1: Define Your Tables

At a minimum, your project management base should include the following tables:

1. **Projects**
   - Tracks high-level information about each project.
   - Key fields: Project Name, Description, Start Date, End Date, Status, Assigned Team.
2. **Tasks**
   - Tracks individual tasks associated with projects.
   - Key fields: Task Name, Assigned To, Due Date, Priority, Status, Linked Project.
3. **Team Members**
   - Stores information about team members involved in the projects.
   - Key fields: Name, Role, Contact Information, Linked Tasks.

Step 2: Create Key Fields

In your tables, use appropriate field types to capture essential details:

- **Single Select Fields**: Use for statuses like "To Do," "In Progress," and "Completed."
- **Date Fields**: Use for start and due dates to enable timeline tracking.
- **Linked Fields**: Link tasks to their corresponding projects and team members.
- **Attachment Fields**: Store project-related files, such as briefs or designs.

Organizing Tasks with Views

Airtable's views allow you to filter, sort, and group tasks in various ways to improve visibility.

1. Kanban View

- Group tasks by status (e.g., "To Do," "In Progress," "Completed").
- Use drag-and-drop functionality to move tasks between statuses.

2. Calendar View

- Display tasks by due dates.
- Identify overlapping deadlines or bottlenecks.

3. Grid View

- Create a detailed list of all tasks.
- Sort or filter tasks by priority, assigned team member, or project.

4. Timeline View

- Visualize tasks along a timeline to track dependencies and progress.
- Ideal for Gantt chart-style project management.

Automating Task Management

1. Task Notifications

Set up automations to notify team members when tasks are assigned to them.

Example Automation:

- **Trigger**: When a record is updated (e.g., Task Status changes to "In Progress").
- **Action**: Send an email to the assigned team member with task details.

2. Due Date Reminders

Ensure tasks are completed on time with automatic reminders.

Example Automation:

- **Trigger**: When the due date is approaching (e.g., 2 days before).
- **Action**: Send a Slack or email reminder to the task owner.

3. Status Updates

Automatically update project statuses based on task progress.

Example Automation:

- **Trigger**: When all linked tasks are marked as "Completed."
- **Action**: Update the project's status to "Completed."

Collaborating with Your Team

1. Sharing and Permissions

- Share the base with team members and assign appropriate permissions (e.g., editor, commenter, read-only).
- Use shared views for external stakeholders to provide project updates without allowing edits.

2. Comments and Attachments

- Use record comments for real-time discussions.
- Attach relevant files or documents directly to records for easy access.

3. Activity Log

- Monitor changes made to tasks or projects using the revision history.

Advanced Features for Project Management

1. Custom Dashboards

Use Airtable apps like Chart or Summary to create a project dashboard:

- Visualize the number of tasks in each status.
- Track progress with a percentage completion chart.

2. Dependency Tracking

- Use linked fields and formula fields to identify dependencies between tasks.
- Ensure tasks are completed in the correct sequence.

3. Resource Management

- Monitor team workloads by grouping tasks by assigned team member.
- Identify over-allocated resources and redistribute tasks as needed.

Example: Managing a Marketing Campaign

Step 1: Set Up Tables

1. **Projects Table**:
   - Example Project: "Product Launch Campaign."
2. **Tasks Table**:
   - Task 1: "Design Ad Creatives"
   - Task 2: "Write Press Release"
   - Task 3: "Schedule Social Media Posts"
3. **Team Members Table**:
   - Include names, roles, and tasks assigned to each team member.

Step 2: Automate Notifications

- Notify the designer when the "Design Ad Creatives" task is assigned.
- Send a reminder to the social media manager 2 days before the "Schedule Social Media Posts" deadline.

Step 3: Track Progress

- Use a Kanban view to track the status of each task.
- Update the project's status to "Completed" once all tasks are done.

Tips for Effective Task Tracking

1. Prioritize Tasks

Use a priority field (e.g., "High," "Medium," "Low") to focus on critical tasks first.

2. Regularly Update Statuses

Encourage team members to update task statuses in real time to ensure accurate progress tracking.

3. Review Workloads

Periodically review team members' workloads to prevent burnout and ensure equitable task distribution.

4. Document Workflows

Create a reference guide or onboarding material to standardize task management processes across the team.

Troubleshooting Common Issues

1. Overdue Tasks

- **Cause**: Tasks are not updated regularly or reminders are missed.
- **Solution**: Automate reminders and enforce regular updates from team members.

2. Unclear Responsibilities

- **Cause**: Tasks are not clearly assigned.
- **Solution**: Always specify a responsible team member for each task.

3. Disconnected Tasks and Projects

- **Cause**: Tasks are not linked to their respective projects.
- **Solution**: Use linked fields to establish clear relationships between tasks and projects.

Conclusion

Airtable makes project management and task tracking simple yet powerful. With its customizable tables, views, and automations, you can create a system that adapts to your team's unique needs. By following the best practices outlined in this chapter, you'll ensure your projects stay on track, tasks are completed on time, and your team remains productive.

CRM and Sales Pipelines

Customer Relationship Management (CRM) is the backbone of sales and customer engagement for businesses of all sizes. Airtable's flexibility makes it an excellent platform for building a customized CRM system that fits your unique business processes. By combining data organization, automation, and collaboration, Airtable can help you manage leads, track customer interactions, and optimize your sales pipeline efficiently.

In this chapter, we'll guide you through setting up a CRM and sales pipeline in Airtable, from tracking leads to automating follow-ups. Whether you're managing a small team or a large sales organization, these strategies will help you streamline your operations and close deals faster.

Setting Up a CRM in Airtable

Step 1: Define Your Tables

Your CRM should include these core tables:

1. **Leads**
   - Tracks potential customers or clients.
   - Key fields: Name, Contact Information, Source, Status, Linked Opportunities.
2. **Opportunities**
   - Tracks potential deals or sales associated with leads.
   - Key fields: Opportunity Name, Value, Stage, Linked Lead, Close Date.
3. **Contacts**
   - Stores information about key decision-makers and stakeholders.
   - Key fields: Name, Role, Email, Phone, Linked Company or Lead.
4. **Interactions**
   - Logs communications and interactions with leads and customers.
   - Key fields: Interaction Date, Type (Email, Call, Meeting), Notes, Linked Lead or Contact.

Step 2: Create Key Fields

Use the following field types to ensure your CRM captures all necessary details:

- **Single Select Fields**: Use for lead status (e.g., New, Contacted, Qualified, Lost) or opportunity stage (e.g., Discovery, Proposal, Negotiation, Closed-Won).
- **Currency Fields**: Track the potential value of deals.
- **Date Fields**: Record important dates, such as interaction dates or deal close dates.
- **Linked Fields**: Connect related tables, such as linking leads to their opportunities or interactions.

Designing a Sales Pipeline

1. Track Lead Status

- Use the **Leads** table to organize leads by status, such as:
  - **New**: Recently added leads.
  - **Contacted**: Initial outreach completed.
  - **Qualified**: Determined as a potential customer.
  - **Lost**: Not moving forward.

2. Manage Opportunity Stages

- Use the **Opportunities** table to track the progression of deals through stages:
  - Discovery
  - Proposal Sent
  - Negotiation
  - Closed-Won
  - Closed-Lost

3. Visualize the Pipeline

- Use a **Kanban View** in the Opportunities table to group deals by stage and drag-and-drop them as they progress.
- Use a **Timeline View** to track close dates and ensure timely follow-ups.

Automating CRM Workflows

1. Lead Assignment

Automatically assign new leads to sales representatives based on criteria like location or deal size.

Example Automation:

- **Trigger**: When a new lead is added.
- **Action**: Update the "Assigned To" field with the appropriate team member.

2. Follow-Up Reminders

Send reminders to sales reps to follow up with leads at specific intervals.

Example Automation:

- **Trigger**: When the "Last Interaction" field is updated.
- **Action**: Send a reminder email or Slack notification after 3 days.

3. Opportunity Notifications

Notify team members when an opportunity progresses to a critical stage.

Example Automation:

- **Trigger**: When an opportunity moves to the "Negotiation" stage.
- **Action**: Notify the assigned rep and their manager via email.

Analyzing CRM Performance

1. Sales Metrics Dashboard

Use Airtable apps like the Chart App to create a dashboard that visualizes key metrics, such as:

- Number of leads in each status.
- Total value of opportunities in the pipeline.
- Conversion rates from lead to closed deal.

2. Revenue Projections

Use formula fields in the Opportunities table to calculate potential revenue based on deal probability.

3. Team Performance Tracking

- Group opportunities by assigned sales rep to track individual performance.
- Monitor metrics like deals closed and total revenue generated.

Advanced Features for CRM

1. Email Integration

- Use apps like the Gmail or Outlook integration to log emails automatically as interactions.
- Send emails directly from Airtable using the SendGrid app.

2. Custom Reports

- Use the Page Designer app to generate professional reports or summaries for leads and opportunities.

3. Third-Party Integrations

- Integrate with tools like Salesforce, HubSpot, or Zapier to expand your CRM's capabilities.

Real-World Example: Managing a Sales Pipeline

Scenario

A software company wants to manage its sales pipeline in Airtable, tracking leads, deals, and interactions.

Step 1: Set Up Tables

1. **Leads Table**:
   - Example Lead: "John Doe, ABC Corp."
2. **Opportunities Table**:
   - Example Opportunity: "ABC Corp - SaaS Subscription" (Value: $5,000).
3. **Interactions Table**:
   - Example Interaction: "Call with John Doe on January 15th."

Step 2: Automate Workflows

- Automatically assign leads based on territory.
- Send reminders to follow up with leads every 5 days.

Step 3: Analyze Performance

- Use a sales dashboard to track total pipeline value and individual rep performance.

Best Practices for CRM Success

1. Standardize Data Entry

Use single select fields and predefined templates to ensure consistent data entry.

2. Regularly Update Statuses

Encourage sales reps to update lead and opportunity statuses frequently to maintain accuracy.

3. Review Interactions Regularly

Ensure all interactions are logged to track the history of communication with each lead.

4. Train Your Team

Provide training on using Airtable for CRM to ensure team members understand workflows and best practices.

Troubleshooting Common CRM Issues

1. Missing Data

- **Cause**: Team members forget to log interactions.
- **Solution**: Use automations to send reminders after meetings or calls.

2. Overlapping Responsibilities

- **Cause**: Multiple sales reps working on the same lead.
- **Solution**: Assign a single owner for each lead or opportunity.

3. Inconsistent Updates

- **Cause**: Leads and opportunities are not updated regularly.
- **Solution**: Conduct weekly pipeline reviews with the team.

Conclusion

Airtable provides the tools you need to build an efficient and flexible CRM system. By setting up a well-structured base, leveraging automations, and analyzing key metrics, you can streamline your sales pipeline and improve customer engagement.

Content Calendar and Editorial Planning

Content creation requires careful planning, coordination, and execution, especially when managing multiple projects, contributors, or platforms. Airtable provides a dynamic and customizable way to manage content calendars and editorial workflows. By centralizing all aspects of content planning—from ideation to publication—you can streamline processes, enhance collaboration, and ensure consistent quality and delivery.

In this chapter, you'll learn how to use Airtable to create and manage a robust content calendar, track editorial tasks, and optimize your workflow to meet publishing deadlines.

Setting Up Your Content Calendar

Step 1: Define Your Tables

A comprehensive content calendar in Airtable typically includes these tables:

1. **Content Calendar**
   - Tracks all pieces of content in your pipeline.
   - Key fields: Content Title, Status, Publish Date, Assigned Contributor, Platform, Linked Campaign.
2. **Campaigns**
   - Tracks broader campaigns that group related content pieces.
   - Key fields: Campaign Name, Start Date, End Date, Goals, Linked Content.
3. **Contributors**
   - Stores details about writers, designers, or other team members involved in content production.
   - Key fields: Name, Role, Contact Information, Linked Tasks.
4. **Tasks**
   - Breaks down content production into specific tasks.
   - Key fields: Task Name, Assigned To, Due Date, Status, Linked Content.

Step 2: Create Key Fields

Set up fields to capture essential details:

- **Single Select Fields**: Use for content status (e.g., Draft, In Review, Scheduled, Published).
- **Date Fields**: Track deadlines, publish dates, and campaign timelines.
- **Linked Fields**: Connect content pieces to campaigns, contributors, or tasks.
- **Attachment Fields**: Store drafts, graphics, or other assets directly within the record.

Organizing Your Content Calendar

1. Calendar View

- Display content pieces by publish date.
- Identify gaps or overlaps in your schedule.

2. Kanban View

- Group content by status to visualize your workflow (e.g., Draft, Review, Published).

- Drag and drop content to update statuses easily.

3. Grid View

- Maintain a detailed list of all content.
- Filter by platform, campaign, or contributor to focus on specific areas.

4. Timeline View

- Track campaign timelines or content deadlines to ensure everything aligns with overarching goals.

Workflow Automation

1. Automated Status Updates

Update content status automatically based on task completion.

Example Automation:

- **Trigger**: When all linked tasks for a content piece are marked "Completed."
- **Action**: Update the content status to "Ready for Review."

2. Publish Date Reminders

Send notifications to contributors as deadlines approach.

Example Automation:

- **Trigger**: When the publish date is 2 days away.
- **Action**: Send an email reminder to the assigned contributor.

3. Editorial Task Assignments

Assign tasks automatically based on content type.

Example Automation:

- **Trigger**: When a new content record is created with "Blog Post" as the type.
- **Action**: Assign the writing task to the content writer automatically.

Tracking Editorial Progress

1. Status Tracking

- Use single select fields to track the progress of each content piece (e.g., Idea, Draft, In Review, Scheduled, Published).
- Combine with color-coding in Kanban or Calendar views for better visualization.

2. Contributor Workload

- Group tasks by assigned contributors to ensure workloads are balanced.
- Monitor progress and reassign tasks if deadlines are at risk.

3. Feedback and Revisions

- Use the comment feature to provide feedback directly on content records.

- Track revision history to ensure feedback is implemented.

Advanced Features for Content Management

1. Integration with Publishing Platforms

- Integrate Airtable with tools like WordPress or social media schedulers (e.g., Buffer or Hootsuite) to publish content directly.
- Automate status updates when content is published.

2. Content Metrics Dashboard

- Use Airtable's apps to create a dashboard tracking content performance, such as views, shares, or engagement rates.
- Link performance metrics back to campaigns for deeper insights.

3. Asset Library

- Create a table to store reusable assets like graphics, templates, or videos.
- Link assets to their respective content pieces for quick access.

Real-World Example: Managing a Blog Content Calendar

Scenario

A marketing team wants to manage their blog publishing schedule and ensure consistency across multiple writers and deadlines.

Step 1: Set Up Tables

1. **Content Calendar Table**:
   - Example: "How to Optimize Your Workflow."
   - Fields: Publish Date, Status, Assigned Writer, Campaign (e.g., Productivity Month).
2. **Contributors Table**:
   - List of writers with their roles and tasks.
3. **Tasks Table**:
   - Example: "Write Draft for 'How to Optimize Your Workflow.'"

Step 2: Automate Workflows

- Notify the writer when the draft is due.
- Update the blog status to "In Review" once the draft is completed.

Step 3: Track Progress

- Use a Kanban view to track the status of all blog posts.
- Review workload distribution by grouping tasks by contributor.

Best Practices for Content Calendar Management

1. Plan Ahead

- Schedule content at least one month in advance to avoid last-minute rushes.

2. Standardize Processes

- Use templates for common content types (e.g., blog posts, social media campaigns) to ensure consistency.

3. Collaborate Effectively

- Use Airtable's commenting feature to provide clear and actionable feedback on drafts.

4. Regularly Review Performance

- Analyze content performance to refine your strategy and focus on high-performing formats or topics.

Troubleshooting Common Issues

1. Missed Deadlines

- **Cause**: Overlooked tasks or mismanaged workloads.
- **Solution**: Automate reminders and review workloads regularly.

2. Duplicated Content

- **Cause**: Lack of centralization.
- **Solution**: Use Airtable to track all content and prevent duplication.

3. Inconsistent Quality

- **Cause**: Varying processes across contributors.
- **Solution**: Standardize workflows and provide clear guidelines for each content type.

Conclusion

Airtable's versatility makes it an excellent choice for managing content calendars and editorial planning. By leveraging its views, automations, and integrations, you can create a streamlined workflow that ensures timely, high-quality content production.

Inventory Management and Asset Tracking

Managing inventory and tracking assets effectively are crucial for businesses of all sizes, ensuring that resources are available when needed and minimizing operational disruptions. Airtable provides a flexible, customizable solution for inventory management and asset tracking, enabling you to create a system tailored to your specific requirements.

In this chapter, we'll explore how to use Airtable to manage your inventory, track assets, and maintain a clear overview of stock levels, locations, and usage. Whether you're running a small business, managing equipment, or overseeing a warehouse, Airtable can streamline your processes and improve efficiency.

Setting Up Your Inventory and Asset Tracking Base

Step 1: Define Your Tables

A typical inventory and asset tracking base might include the following tables:

1. **Inventory**
   - Tracks all inventory items, such as products, raw materials, or consumables.
   - Key fields: Item Name, SKU, Category, Stock Level, Reorder Level, Location.
2. **Assets**
   - Tracks physical or digital assets, such as equipment, vehicles, or software licenses.
   - Key fields: Asset Name, Asset Type, Serial Number, Purchase Date, Status, Location.
3. **Suppliers**
   - Stores information about suppliers or vendors for inventory replenishment.
   - Key fields: Supplier Name, Contact Information, Linked Items.
4. **Transactions**
   - Logs stock movements, such as purchases, sales, or transfers.
   - Key fields: Item, Transaction Type (e.g., Add, Remove), Quantity, Date, Notes.
5. **Locations**
   - Tracks storage locations, such as warehouses, shelves, or offices.
   - Key fields: Location Name, Address, Linked Items.

Step 2: Create Key Fields

Use the following field types to capture essential data:

- **Single Select Fields**: Use for item categories, asset statuses (e.g., Active, In Use, Under Maintenance), or transaction types.
- **Number Fields**: Track stock levels, quantities, and reorder points.
- **Date Fields**: Record purchase dates or transaction dates.
- **Linked Fields**: Connect related tables, such as items to suppliers or assets to locations.
- **Attachment Fields**: Store photos or documents related to items or assets.

Organizing and Visualizing Inventory

1. Grid View

- Maintain a detailed list of all inventory items and their current stock levels.
- Use filters to view items below their reorder level or in specific categories.

2. Kanban View

- Group assets or items by status (e.g., Active, In Maintenance, Retired).
- Drag and drop items to update their status easily.

3. Calendar View

- Track asset maintenance schedules or restocking dates.

4. Timeline View

- Visualize asset usage over time, ensuring optimal resource allocation.

Automating Inventory and Asset Workflows

1. Low Stock Alerts

Receive notifications when inventory levels fall below the reorder point.

Example Automation:

- **Trigger**: When the "Stock Level" field is less than or equal to the "Reorder Level" field.
- **Action**: Send an email to the purchasing team with item details.

2. Maintenance Reminders

Set reminders for routine asset maintenance.

Example Automation:

- **Trigger**: When the "Next Maintenance Date" is approaching.
- **Action**: Notify the asset manager with a maintenance checklist.

3. Transaction Logging

Automatically update stock levels based on transactions.

Example Automation:

- **Trigger**: When a new transaction record is created.
- **Action**: Adjust the stock level in the linked inventory record.

Tracking Asset Usage and Status

1. Status Monitoring

- Use a single select field to track asset statuses, such as Active, In Use, Maintenance, or Retired.
- Combine with color-coding in Kanban views for a quick visual overview.

2. Usage History

- Use the Transactions table to log the usage history of each asset, such as check-ins, check-outs, or repairs.
- Link transactions to the corresponding asset record for detailed tracking.

3. Depreciation Tracking

- Add formula fields to calculate asset depreciation over time based on purchase date and lifespan.

Analyzing Inventory and Asset Data

1. Inventory Levels Dashboard

Use Airtable apps like Chart or Summary to create dashboards:

- Visualize total stock levels by category.
- Identify items with low stock levels or high turnover rates.

2. Supplier Performance

Analyze supplier data to identify trends, such as delivery reliability or cost changes.

3. Asset Utilization

Track the frequency of asset usage to identify underutilized resources or plan replacements.

Real-World Example: Managing IT Equipment

Scenario

An IT department wants to track all equipment, monitor stock levels for consumables, and schedule maintenance for assets.

Step 1: Set Up Tables

1. **Assets Table**:
   - Example Asset: "Dell Latitude 5420 Laptop."
   - Fields: Serial Number, Status, Purchase Date, Linked Transactions.
2. **Transactions Table**:
   - Example Transaction: "Laptop issued to John Doe on January 15th."
3. **Suppliers Table**:
   - Example Supplier: "Tech Supplies Co."

Step 2: Automate Workflows

- Notify the IT manager when laptops are due for maintenance.
- Alert the purchasing team when printer ink stock is low.

Step 3: Analyze Data

- Use a dashboard to track asset usage and identify underutilized equipment.

Best Practices for Inventory and Asset Management

1. Standardize Data Entry

Use predefined options in single select fields to maintain consistency.

2. Regularly Audit Inventory

Conduct periodic checks to ensure data accuracy and identify discrepancies.

3. Optimize Reordering

Set realistic reorder levels based on usage trends to avoid overstocking or stockouts.

4. Centralize Data

Store all inventory and asset data in a single Airtable base to improve accessibility and reduce duplication.

Troubleshooting Common Issues

1. Stock Discrepancies

- **Cause**: Unrecorded transactions or manual errors.
- **Solution**: Automate transaction logging and conduct regular audits.

2. Asset Misplacement

- **Cause**: Lack of location tracking.
- **Solution**: Use the Locations table and ensure all assets are tagged with their location.

3. Missed Maintenance

- **Cause**: No reminders for routine maintenance.
- **Solution**: Automate maintenance schedules and reminders.

Conclusion

Airtable provides a flexible and scalable solution for inventory management and asset tracking. By setting up structured tables, automating workflows, and leveraging visualizations, you can optimize operations, reduce errors, and make data-driven decisions.

Section 10:
Best Practices and Maintenance

Data Backup and Recovery Strategies

Data is one of the most critical assets of any organization. Ensuring that your Airtable data is backed up and easily recoverable in case of loss, corruption, or accidental deletion is essential. While Airtable provides a certain level of built-in redundancy and recovery options, implementing a robust backup and recovery strategy is vital for long-term data security and peace of mind.

This chapter will guide you through the best practices for data backup and recovery, the tools Airtable provides for these purposes, and additional strategies you can adopt to safeguard your data.

Why Backup and Recovery Are Important

1. Protect Against Data Loss

Accidental deletions, overwriting, or errors during data imports can lead to loss of valuable information.

2. Ensure Business Continuity

In critical operations, having readily available backups ensures minimal disruption in case of data loss.

3. Maintain Historical Data

Backups help retain historical records for auditing, analysis, or compliance purposes.

4. Prepare for Scaling

As your Airtable bases grow and involve more collaborators, the risk of errors increases, making backups more critical.

Airtable's Built-In Backup Features

1. Revision History

- Airtable automatically tracks changes to your base for up to **one year** on Pro and Enterprise plans.
- Revision history allows you to see changes made by collaborators and revert to previous states.

How to Use:

- Click the **"History"** button in the upper-right corner of the base.
- Review edits and restore previous versions if needed.

2. Snapshots

- Airtable's snapshot feature automatically saves point-in-time copies of your base.
- Snapshots can be restored to recover data from a specific point.

How to Use:

- Navigate to the base settings.
- Open the **"Snapshots"** tab.
- Choose a snapshot to restore.

3. Trash Recovery

- Deleted records and fields can be restored within a limited timeframe.
- This feature prevents accidental loss of recently deleted data.

How to Use:

- Look for the notification banner after deletion.
- Click **"Undo"** or navigate to the **trash bin** for recovery.

Advanced Backup Strategies

While Airtable's built-in features provide a level of security, it's essential to implement additional strategies for comprehensive protection.

1. Manual CSV Exports

Regularly export your Airtable data to CSV files as a basic backup strategy.

Steps:

- Open your base and select the desired table.
- Click the **"View options"** menu and choose **"Download CSV."**
- Store the exported file securely, preferably in a cloud storage service like Google Drive or Dropbox.

2. Use Third-Party Backup Tools

Several third-party tools offer automated backups for Airtable bases, making the process seamless and consistent.

Popular Tools:

- **On2Air Backups**: Automates Airtable backups and stores them securely in cloud platforms.
- **Zapier**: Use Airtable-Zapier integrations to create workflows for data exports to Google Sheets or other storage solutions.

3. Integrate with Cloud Storage Services

Sync your Airtable data with platforms like Google Drive or OneDrive to maintain regular backups.

Example Workflow:

- Set up an integration (using tools like Zapier or Make) to export records to a Google Sheet daily.

4. API-Based Backups

For larger teams or advanced users, use Airtable's API to build a custom backup system.

Steps:

- Use the Airtable API to pull data from your bases.

- Store the data in your own database or cloud storage.
- Schedule regular backup runs using automation tools like Python scripts or cloud-based cron jobs.

Recovery Strategies

1. Restoring from Snapshots

Snapshots are the quickest way to recover your base to a previous state. Ensure that team members know how to access and use snapshots for recovery.

2. Importing Backups

If you've exported data as CSV files or synced it to external systems, you can reimport this data into Airtable.

Steps:

- Create a new base or table.
- Use the **"Import CSV"** feature to upload your backup file.
- Recreate any formulas, views, or relationships manually, if needed.

3. Collaborative Communication

If an error or loss occurs due to collaboration issues, use Airtable's revision history to identify the source of the problem and involve relevant collaborators in the recovery process.

Best Practices for Airtable Data Backup

1. Schedule Regular Backups

- Back up critical bases at least once a week, or more frequently for active projects.

2. Create a Backup Policy

- Define who is responsible for backups and how often they should occur.

3. Test Recovery Procedures

- Periodically test your recovery strategy to ensure it works as expected.

4. Secure Backup Storage

- Encrypt backup files and use platforms with strong security measures for storage.

5. Document Backup Processes

- Maintain documentation on how backups are created, where they are stored, and how to recover data.

Troubleshooting Common Backup and Recovery Issues

1. Missing or Incomplete Backups

- **Cause**: Irregular backups or partial exports.

- **Solution**: Automate backups using third-party tools to ensure completeness.

2. Conflicts During Recovery

- **Cause**: Reimporting data into a base with existing, conflicting records.
- **Solution**: Use unique identifiers (e.g., IDs or SKUs) to match and update records correctly.

3. Overwritten Data

- **Cause**: Human error during collaboration.
- **Solution**: Use revision history or snapshots to restore data to its original state.

Real-World Example: Backup for a Retail Business

Scenario

A retail business uses Airtable to track inventory and sales. They want to ensure their data is safe from accidental deletions or errors.

Backup Strategy

1. **Manual Backups**: Export inventory and sales data to CSV weekly.
2. **Automated Backups**: Use On2Air to back up data to Google Drive daily.
3. **Snapshots**: Enable regular snapshots for quick recovery.

Recovery Plan

1. Restore the inventory base from a recent snapshot.
2. Use manual CSV backups to fill gaps in data if needed.

Conclusion

A robust data backup and recovery strategy is essential for maintaining the integrity of your Airtable data. By leveraging Airtable's built-in features, automating backups, and implementing recovery workflows, you can ensure that your data is secure and accessible when needed.

Security and Compliance in Airtable

As businesses and organizations increasingly rely on Airtable to manage sensitive data and workflows, ensuring data security and compliance with industry standards becomes a top priority. Airtable offers robust security features to safeguard your data, but understanding how to leverage these tools effectively and adhering to compliance requirements are crucial for protecting your organization.

This chapter will explore Airtable's security features, compliance capabilities, and best practices for maintaining a secure environment. Whether you're handling sensitive client information or internal business data, these strategies will help you meet security and compliance expectations.

Airtable's Built-In Security Features

1. Data Encryption

Airtable employs encryption to protect data both in transit and at rest.

- **In Transit**: Airtable uses TLS (Transport Layer Security) to encrypt data as it travels between your devices and Airtable servers.
- **At Rest**: All data stored on Airtable's servers is encrypted using AES-256, an industry-standard encryption protocol.

2. User Authentication

Airtable supports secure user authentication options:

- **Single Sign-On (SSO)**: Available on Enterprise plans, SSO integrates with identity providers like Okta, Google Workspace, and Azure AD.
- **Two-Factor Authentication (2FA)**: Adds an additional layer of security by requiring a verification code during login.

3. Role-Based Permissions

Airtable provides granular control over who can access and modify data:

- **Base-Level Permissions**: Restrict access to specific bases for individual users or teams.
- **Collaborator Roles**: Assign roles such as Owner, Editor, Commenter, or Read-Only to collaborators.
- **Field and Table Permissions**: Limit access to specific fields or tables within a base.

4. Audit Logs and Activity Tracking

Pro and Enterprise plans include activity logs to track changes:

- Monitor who accessed or modified data.
- View timestamps for each action.

5. Backup and Recovery

Airtable automatically creates snapshots of your bases, which can be restored if data is lost or corrupted.

Compliance Standards Supported by Airtable

Airtable complies with key industry standards to ensure data protection:

1. SOC 2 Type II Certification

Airtable is certified for **SOC 2 Type II**, demonstrating adherence to strict security, availability, and confidentiality requirements.

2. GDPR Compliance

For organizations handling data from the European Union, Airtable complies with the **General Data Protection Regulation (GDPR)**, offering tools to manage and protect personal data.

3. HIPAA Compliance

With the Enterprise plan, Airtable offers **HIPAA-compliant features** for managing sensitive health information, including signed Business Associate Agreements (BAAs).

4. CCPA Compliance

Airtable adheres to the **California Consumer Privacy Act (CCPA)**, ensuring data privacy and transparency for California residents.

Implementing Best Practices for Security

1. Strengthen User Authentication

- Enable **Two-Factor Authentication (2FA)** for all users.
- Use strong, unique passwords for Airtable accounts.
- For Enterprise users, implement **Single Sign-On (SSO)** for centralized user management.

2. Use Role-Based Access Control

- Assign permissions based on the principle of least privilege, ensuring users only have access to the data they need.
- Regularly review and update permissions to remove unnecessary access.

3. Monitor Activity Logs

- Use Airtable's activity logs to track user actions and identify potential unauthorized access or changes.

4. Encrypt Sensitive Data

While Airtable provides encryption, you can further secure sensitive information:

- Use third-party encryption tools to encrypt data before uploading it to Airtable.
- Avoid storing unencrypted passwords, financial information, or sensitive personal data in Airtable.

5. Automate Security Workflows

Set up automated notifications to flag potential security breaches:

- Use Airtable Automations to trigger alerts when sensitive data is accessed or modified.

Maintaining Compliance in Airtable

1. Understand Your Regulatory Requirements

Identify the compliance standards applicable to your organization, such as GDPR, HIPAA, or CCPA.

2. Use Airtable's Compliance Tools

Leverage Airtable's built-in features for managing compliance:

- **Data Export**: Export data for audits or compliance reporting.
- **Data Deletion**: Use Airtable's deletion tools to remove personal data when requested.

3. Secure Data Transfers

If you're integrating Airtable with third-party tools, ensure data is transferred securely using encryption and secure APIs.

4. Document Compliance Practices

Maintain detailed records of your Airtable security and compliance policies to demonstrate adherence during audits.

Troubleshooting Common Security Issues

1. Unauthorized Access

- **Cause**: Weak passwords or misconfigured permissions.
- **Solution**: Strengthen passwords, enable 2FA, and review access permissions regularly.

2. Data Breaches

- **Cause**: Phishing attacks or unencrypted sensitive data.
- **Solution**: Train users on security best practices and avoid storing sensitive data unencrypted.

3. Incomplete Data Deletion

- **Cause**: Retention of data in archived or hidden fields.
- **Solution**: Ensure data is deleted across all fields and backups.

Real-World Example: Securing a Client Database

Scenario

A marketing agency uses Airtable to manage client projects, including sensitive client data. They want to enhance security to protect client confidentiality.

Solution

1. Enable 2FA for all collaborators.
2. Assign Read-Only permissions to clients and editors.
3. Automate alerts for changes to sensitive fields, such as budget or client contact details.
4. Regularly export and encrypt backups for compliance with GDPR.

Future-Proofing Airtable Security

1. Stay Informed

Keep up-to-date with Airtable's latest security features and industry compliance standards.

2. Regular Security Audits

Periodically audit your Airtable bases for potential security risks or non-compliance.

3. Invest in Training

Educate your team on Airtable's security features and best practices to minimize human error.

Conclusion

By leveraging Airtable's robust security features and implementing best practices, you can safeguard your data and meet industry compliance standards. Whether protecting sensitive client information or internal records, prioritizing security ensures peace of mind and operational continuity.

Scaling Up: Handling Larger Teams and Bases

As your organization grows, so do the demands on your Airtable setup. Managing larger teams and bases requires a strategic approach to ensure efficiency, maintain data integrity, and prevent bottlenecks. Airtable is built to scale, but it's essential to implement best practices for managing collaboration, organizing data, and optimizing performance.

In this chapter, we'll explore strategies for scaling Airtable to accommodate larger teams and more complex bases. From structuring bases to managing permissions, these tips will help you maintain a seamless workflow as your needs expand.

Structuring Your Base for Scalability

1. Plan Your Base Architecture

- **Break Down Complex Data**: Instead of cramming everything into a single table, use linked tables to manage related data.
- **Use Consistent Naming Conventions**: Standardize table, field, and record names to avoid confusion as your team grows.
- **Group Data by Function**: Organize tables by functional areas, such as projects, clients, or teams, to keep data manageable.

2. Optimize Field Usage

- **Limit Field Types**: Avoid excessive use of formula or linked fields that can slow down performance.
- **Archive Unused Fields**: Regularly review and archive fields that are no longer relevant.

3. Leverage Views for Clarity

- **Create Team-Specific Views**: Customize views for different roles or departments to reduce clutter.
- **Use Filters**: Apply filters to show only the most relevant records for each team or project.

Managing Larger Teams

1. Use Role-Based Permissions

- Assign collaborators specific roles (Owner, Editor, Commenter, Read-Only) to control who can view or modify data.
- Set **table-level permissions** for sensitive information to prevent unauthorized access.

2. Establish Collaboration Guidelines

- **Document Processes**: Create a manual or guide for team members on how to interact with bases.
- **Use Comments Effectively**: Encourage teams to use Airtable's comment feature for communication instead of editing data directly.
- **Track Changes**: Use Airtable's activity log to monitor who made changes and when.

3. Automate Notifications

Set up Airtable Automations to notify teams of updates, approvals, or new tasks to streamline communication.

Optimizing Performance

1. Reduce Base Size

- Archive old records or create a separate base for historical data to keep the main base responsive.
- Limit the number of linked records and large attachments.

2. Monitor Formula Fields

- Simplify complex formulas to avoid slowing down performance.
- Replace redundant formulas with static fields when possible.

3. Use Batch Operations

For large updates, use Airtable's bulk editing features or integrate with tools like Zapier for automated batch processing.

4. Test Base Performance

Regularly test your base for performance issues by monitoring loading times and user feedback.

Integrating with Third-Party Tools

1. Use Airtable API

For advanced scalability, integrate Airtable with custom applications or external systems using its robust API.

2. Employ Automation Platforms

- Use tools like Zapier, Make (formerly Integromat), or Workato to automate workflows and reduce manual tasks.
- Integrate with communication tools like Slack or Microsoft Teams to keep your team updated.

3. Backup and Sync Data

- Use third-party tools to back up Airtable data to cloud storage solutions like Google Drive or AWS.
- Sync Airtable with other databases or CRMs for real-time data sharing.

Scaling Collaboration

1. Group Users into Teams

- Organize users into teams within Airtable's workspace settings to streamline access and permissions.
- Use shared team workspaces to centralize collaboration.

2. Implement a Review Process

- Set up approval workflows to ensure data accuracy before it's finalized.
- Use the "Lock Views" feature to prevent changes to specific views or data sets.

3. Create Dashboards

Build summary dashboards for team leads or executives to provide an overview of key metrics and data trends.

Troubleshooting Common Challenges

1. Overwhelming Base Complexity

- **Cause**: Too many tables, fields, or views in a single base.
- **Solution**: Split the base into multiple bases for different departments or purposes and use synced tables to connect them.

2. Permissions Confusion

- **Cause**: Mismanagement of user roles and permissions.
- **Solution**: Review permissions regularly and simplify roles based on team functions.

3. Data Loss or Overwrites

- **Cause**: Multiple users editing the same records simultaneously.
- **Solution**: Use Airtable's revision history to track and restore changes.

4. Slow Performance

- **Cause**: Large datasets or complex formulas.
- **Solution**: Optimize formulas, archive old data, and minimize the use of linked records.

Real-World Example: Scaling a Marketing Agency

Scenario

A marketing agency expands from a 5-person team to a 50-person operation, requiring better organization and scalability in Airtable.

Solution

1. **Base Organization**: Split the original base into separate bases for clients, campaigns, and finances. Use synced tables to connect them.
2. **Team Collaboration**: Assign Editor roles to team leads and Read-Only roles to interns for controlled access.
3. **Automations**: Set up automated notifications for task assignments and campaign deadlines.
4. **Dashboards**: Create high-level dashboards to track campaign performance and team productivity.

Future-Proofing Airtable for Growth

1. Regular Reviews

- Schedule periodic reviews of your Airtable setup to identify and address inefficiencies.

2. Continuous Training

- Train new team members on Airtable best practices to ensure consistency.

3. Explore New Features

- Stay updated on Airtable's latest features, such as interface updates or expanded automation capabilities.

Conclusion

Scaling Airtable for larger teams and bases requires careful planning, regular maintenance, and leveraging the platform's advanced features. By structuring bases effectively, optimizing performance, and managing teams with precision, you can ensure Airtable remains a powerful tool for your organization, regardless of size.

Documentation and Team Training

Effective documentation and team training are vital for ensuring consistency, efficiency, and seamless collaboration within your Airtable environment. As your team grows or processes evolve, having a clear set of guidelines and resources can help avoid confusion and ensure everyone is aligned with the system's goals and operations.

In this chapter, we'll explore strategies for creating and maintaining Airtable documentation and providing meaningful training for your team. Whether you're onboarding new members or adapting to process changes, these practices will set the foundation for a well-informed and productive team.

Creating Comprehensive Documentation

1. Define the Purpose of Documentation

Documentation serves multiple purposes, such as onboarding new members, maintaining data consistency, and ensuring compliance with workflows. Be clear about what your documentation is meant to achieve.

2. Include Key Components

Effective documentation should include:

- **Base Overviews**: A description of each base, its purpose, and how it fits into your organization's workflow.
- **Field Definitions**: A glossary of field names, types, and their intended uses to avoid misuse.
- **Workflow Instructions**: Step-by-step guides for key processes, such as adding records, linking data, or using automations.
- **Permissions and Roles**: Guidelines on who can access or edit different bases, views, and fields.
- **Common Issues and Fixes**: A troubleshooting section to address frequently encountered problems.

3. Use Visual Aids

Incorporate screenshots, diagrams, or videos to enhance clarity. For instance:

- Include labeled screenshots of base layouts to familiarize users with the structure.
- Use flowcharts to explain complex workflows or relationships between tables.

4. Centralize Documentation

Store your documentation in an easily accessible location, such as:

- Airtable's **Base Description** field or a dedicated documentation base.
- Cloud-based platforms like Google Drive or Notion for team-wide access.
- Linked resources within your Airtable interface for contextual help.

5. Keep It Updated

Regularly review and update documentation to reflect changes in workflows, team structure, or Airtable features. Assign a team member to oversee this process to ensure it doesn't fall through the cracks.

Designing Effective Training Programs

1. Identify Team Needs

Tailor your training program to the specific needs of your team:

- For **new hires**, focus on foundational Airtable skills like navigating bases, adding records, and using views.
- For **advanced users**, dive into automation setup, scripting, and integrations.

2. Choose the Right Training Methods

Provide a mix of resources to cater to different learning styles:

- **Live Sessions**: Host virtual or in-person training sessions for hands-on practice and Q&A.
- **Pre-Recorded Tutorials**: Create or share video tutorials for self-paced learning.
- **Interactive Exercises**: Use dummy bases or templates for practice without affecting live data.
- **Written Guides**: Complement video tutorials with written step-by-step instructions.

3. Create Role-Specific Training

Customize training for different team roles:

- **Editors**: Teach them how to add, edit, and delete records while maintaining data accuracy.
- **Viewers**: Focus on navigating views, using filters, and leaving comments.
- **Admins**: Cover advanced topics like managing permissions, creating automations, and troubleshooting.

4. Incorporate Hands-On Practice

Encourage trainees to practice in a sandbox base or a duplicate of a live base. Provide scenarios for them to solve, such as:

- Adding linked records.
- Setting up a simple automation.
- Resolving data inconsistencies.

Encouraging Ongoing Learning

1. Provide Continuous Support

Make it easy for team members to seek help when needed:

- Designate Airtable "champions" or power users within your team as go-to resources.
- Set up a shared communication channel, such as Slack, for questions and discussions.

2. Share Updates and Best Practices

As Airtable introduces new features or your workflows evolve, keep the team informed through:

- Regular team meetings or newsletters highlighting updates and changes.
- Sharing links to Airtable's help articles or community forums.

3. Host Refresher Courses

Periodically revisit training topics to ensure your team stays up-to-date and proficient in using Airtable.

Real-World Example: Streamlining Team Training

Scenario

A company onboarded 20 new employees to its marketing team, which relies on Airtable for campaign tracking. Without documentation or training, employees struggled to navigate the system, resulting in errors and inefficiencies.

Solution

1. The company created an Airtable documentation base, including field definitions, workflows, and troubleshooting tips.
2. It hosted a series of live training sessions, starting with Airtable basics and progressing to advanced automations.
3. Each team member practiced in a sandbox base before working on live data.

Outcome

New hires quickly adapted to Airtable, reducing errors by 50% and improving collaboration within the team.

Tips for Success

- **Keep It Simple**: Avoid overwhelming your team with too much information at once. Focus on essential skills first.
- **Encourage Feedback**: Ask your team for feedback on training sessions and documentation to identify areas for improvement.
- **Leverage Airtable Resources**: Use Airtable's built-in guides, templates, and community forum for additional training support.

Conclusion

Documentation and team training are critical components of a successful Airtable strategy. By investing time in creating clear resources and providing meaningful training, you can empower your team to use Airtable effectively and confidently.

Common Pitfalls to Avoid

As powerful and flexible as Airtable is, users often encounter common pitfalls that can hinder productivity, data accuracy, and overall effectiveness. Knowing these challenges in advance allows you to proactively avoid them and set your team up for success.

In this chapter, we'll explore the most frequent mistakes people make when using Airtable and provide actionable tips to overcome or avoid them entirely. From managing data structure to collaborating with your team, this guide will help you sidestep obstacles and maintain a smooth, efficient workflow.

Poor Base Design

1. Lack of Planning

One of the most common mistakes is diving into Airtable without first mapping out your needs and workflows. A poorly planned base can lead to inefficiencies, redundancies, and errors.

Solution:

- Outline your project requirements before creating your base.
- Identify key tables, fields, and relationships in advance.
- Use a whiteboard or diagram tool to visualize how your data will flow.

2. Overcomplicating Your Structure

Adding too many tables, views, and fields can make your base overwhelming and difficult to navigate.

Solution:

- Keep your base structure as simple as possible while meeting your needs.
- Regularly review your base to consolidate or eliminate unnecessary elements.
- Use linked records to avoid duplicating data across tables.

Mismanaging Fields

3. Using Incorrect Field Types

Choosing the wrong field type can result in inconsistent data and limit functionality. For example, using a single-line text field for dates or numbers can make sorting and calculations impossible.

Solution:

- Familiarize yourself with Airtable's field types (e.g., single-select, number, date, formula).
- Choose field types that align with the type of data you're storing.
- Adjust field types if you notice errors or inefficiencies.

4. Ignoring Field Descriptions

Skipping field descriptions can confuse team members and lead to improper data entry.

Solution:

- Use field descriptions to explain the purpose of each field.
- Include examples or guidelines for data entry in the description.

Data Management Issues

5. Inconsistent Data Entry

Allowing users to enter data in different formats (e.g., "NY" vs. "New York") can lead to confusion and errors.

Solution:

- Use single-select or multi-select fields to standardize entries.
- Set up forms for data entry to ensure consistency.
- Regularly review and clean your data to fix inconsistencies.

6. Lack of Data Validation

Failing to validate data can result in duplicate or inaccurate records.

Solution:

- Use automations or formulas to flag duplicates or incorrect entries.
- Leverage Airtable's validation features (e.g., required fields, unique fields).

Collaboration Challenges

7. Overlapping Permissions

Granting too much access to team members can result in accidental data loss or unauthorized changes.

Solution:

- Set permissions based on roles and responsibilities.
- Use read-only or comment-only permissions for users who don't need to edit data.
- Regularly review and adjust permissions as team roles evolve.

8. Lack of Communication

Assuming team members understand your base without proper onboarding can lead to confusion and errors.

Solution:

- Provide clear documentation and training for team members.
- Use comments and descriptions to explain workflows within the base.
- Schedule regular check-ins to address questions and share updates.

Automation and Integration Pitfalls

9. Overloading Automations

Setting up too many automations can cause performance issues and make troubleshooting difficult.

Solution:

- Limit the number of automations by consolidating tasks where possible.
- Test automations in a sandbox base before implementing them in a live base.
- Monitor your automations to ensure they're functioning as intended.

10. Ignoring Third-Party Integration Limits

Integrating Airtable with other tools without understanding their limitations can lead to errors or data sync failures.

Solution:

- Research the integration capabilities and limits of third-party tools.
- Set realistic expectations for what integrations can achieve.
- Monitor integrations regularly to ensure they're working smoothly.

Scaling and Maintenance Issues

11. Not Preparing for Growth

Failing to plan for an increase in data, users, or workflows can lead to bottlenecks and inefficiencies.

Solution:

- Design your base with scalability in mind by using linked records and structured data relationships.
- Periodically archive or delete old records to keep your base manageable.
- Regularly review performance metrics to ensure your base runs smoothly.

12. Neglecting Maintenance

Skipping routine maintenance can result in outdated data, broken workflows, or cluttered bases.

Solution:

- Schedule regular audits to clean up unused fields, views, and tables.
- Update documentation and training materials to reflect changes.
- Back up your data frequently to protect against accidental loss.

Real-World Example: Avoiding Common Pitfalls

Scenario

A marketing team used Airtable for campaign tracking but faced challenges with inconsistent data entry and unclear workflows. Team members often entered data differently, and automations frequently failed due to misconfigurations.

Solution

1. The team restructured their base to standardize field types and reduce redundancy.
2. They provided training sessions for all team members, focusing on best practices for data entry.
3. Automations were streamlined to minimize errors and improve performance.

Outcome

The team reduced data errors by 60% and improved workflow efficiency, allowing them to focus more on campaign execution.

Conclusion

By understanding and addressing these common pitfalls, you can avoid many of the challenges that Airtable users face. Proactively planning your base, managing data effectively, and fostering collaboration within your team will ensure your Airtable workflows remain smooth and efficient.

Appendices

Appendix A: Glossary of Airtable Terms

This glossary provides definitions for key Airtable terms that will help you navigate the platform more effectively. Whether you're a beginner or looking to refine your understanding, this appendix serves as a quick reference guide.

Base

A base is the foundation of your work in Airtable. It is equivalent to a database and contains all the tables, fields, and records related to a specific project or workflow.

Table

A table is a collection of data within a base, organized into rows (records) and columns (fields). Each table typically represents a category of information, such as tasks, contacts, or inventory.

Field

A field is a column in a table, representing a specific attribute or type of information for the records in the table. Examples of fields include names, dates, numbers, or attachments.

Record

A record is a single row in a table, representing an individual item or entry. For example, in a contacts table, each record could represent a single person.

Field Type

Field types define the kind of data a field can hold, such as text, numbers, dates, checkboxes, or attachments. Choosing the correct field type ensures accurate data entry and functionality.

View

A view is a customized way to display and interact with the data in a table. Airtable offers several view types, including grid, calendar, gallery, and kanban. Views help you focus on specific subsets of data or formats.

Linked Record

A linked record connects related information between two tables. This relationship allows you to view and use data from one table in another, avoiding duplication and enhancing organization.

Rollup Field

A rollup field aggregates data from linked records, such as summing numbers, counting entries, or concatenating text. It provides insights and calculations across related tables.

Formula Field

A formula field performs calculations or manipulates data using formulas. These fields are used to generate dynamic content, such as combining text fields or performing date calculations.

Automation

Automations in Airtable enable you to automate repetitive tasks, such as sending notifications, updating records, or triggering integrations with other apps.

Block

Blocks are modular extensions that add advanced functionality to your Airtable base. Examples include charts, maps, and page designer blocks.

Interface

An interface is a customizable, user-friendly layout for interacting with your data. Interfaces are built on top of your base and can include elements like buttons, filters, and charts.

Form

A form is a view designed for data entry. It allows users to input information into a table without needing access to the full base.

Workspace

A workspace is a container for organizing and managing multiple bases. It is commonly used to group related projects or team workflows.

Collaboration

Collaboration refers to Airtable's ability to allow multiple users to work on the same base. Collaboration features include permissions, comments, and shared views.

Revision History

Revision history tracks changes made to records and fields over time. This feature allows you to view, restore, or undo previous versions of your data.

Attachment

An attachment is a type of field that allows you to upload and store files, such as images, PDFs, or documents, directly in your Airtable base.

Filter

A filter is a feature used to display specific records in a table based on defined criteria. Filters help you focus on relevant data.

Group

Grouping organizes records in a table into categories based on a shared field value. For example, you can group tasks by their assigned team member or status.

Color-Coding

Color-coding applies visual markers to records or fields based on defined conditions. It helps highlight important information or statuses.

Sync

Sync allows you to link data between bases or import external data into your base. Changes made to the source data are automatically reflected in the synced base.

API (Application Programming Interface)

The Airtable API enables developers to integrate Airtable with external applications, allowing for custom workflows and automations.

Permissions

Permissions control user access to your base. They allow you to set roles such as creator, editor, commenter, or read-only user to ensure data security.

Kanban View

The kanban view is a type of view that organizes records as cards in columns, typically used for tracking tasks in a project.

Calendar View

The calendar view displays records with date fields on a calendar interface. It's useful for scheduling and timeline management.

Gallery View

The gallery view shows records as cards with a focus on visual elements, such as images or attachments. It's ideal for portfolios or product catalogs.

This glossary is designed to demystify Airtable's terminology and make it easier for you to navigate the platform. Refer back to this whenever you encounter an unfamiliar term, and feel free to expand your understanding as you explore Airtable's features.

Appendix B: Keyboard Shortcuts and Productivity Tips

Mastering Airtable's keyboard shortcuts and leveraging productivity tips can significantly enhance your efficiency and workflow. This appendix provides a comprehensive list of shortcuts and actionable tips to help you work smarter, not harder, within Airtable.

Keyboard Shortcuts for Airtable

General Navigation

- **Cmd + K (Mac) / Ctrl + K (Windows)**: Open the quick find search bar.
- **Cmd + Shift + K (Mac) / Ctrl + Shift + K (Windows)**: Open the recent bases menu.
- **Cmd + 1, 2, etc. (Mac) / Ctrl + 1, 2, etc. (Windows)**: Switch between tabs in your browser.

Table Navigation

- **Arrow Keys**: Move between cells.
- **Tab**: Move to the next cell to the right.
- **Shift + Tab**: Move to the previous cell.
- **Enter**: Open a cell for editing or move to the cell below.
- **Shift + Enter**: Move to the cell above.

Selecting and Editing

- **Cmd + Click (Mac) / Ctrl + Click (Windows)**: Select multiple records or fields.
- **Cmd + C / Cmd + V (Mac) / Ctrl + C / Ctrl + V (Windows)**: Copy and paste cells or fields.
- **Cmd + D (Mac) / Ctrl + D (Windows)**: Duplicate the selected record.

View Management

- **Cmd + Shift + N (Mac) / Ctrl + Shift + N (Windows)**: Create a new view.
- **Cmd + Shift + E (Mac) / Ctrl + Shift + E (Windows)**: Toggle the visibility of hidden fields.

Filtering and Grouping

- **F**: Open the filter menu for the current view.
- **G**: Open the grouping menu for the current view.

Record-Level Actions

- **Space**: Expand a record.
- **Cmd + Delete (Mac) / Ctrl + Delete (Windows)**: Delete a selected record.

Productivity Tips for Airtable

1. Utilize Templates

Airtable offers a variety of pre-built templates tailored to specific use cases, such as project management, CRM, or content calendars. Start with a template to save setup time and customize it to your needs.

2. Create Linked Records

Use linked records to maintain data relationships across tables. For example, link tasks to projects or inventory items to orders, ensuring data consistency and avoiding duplication.

3. Customize Views

- **Filtered Views**: Show only the records you need by applying filters.
- **Grouped Views**: Organize records by specific field values for easy analysis.
- **Color-Coded Views**: Apply color coding based on field conditions to highlight priorities or statuses.

4. Automate Repetitive Tasks

Use Airtable's automation features to send notifications, update records, or integrate with third-party services. Automations reduce manual work and ensure tasks are completed on time.

5. Leverage Formulas

- Use formula fields for calculations, text concatenation, or logical operations.
- Examples:
  - `IF(Status = "Done", "■", "✗")` to track task completion.
  - `DATETIME_DIFF({Due Date}, TODAY(), "days")` to calculate the number of days until a deadline.

6. Use Blocks for Advanced Functionality

Explore Airtable's blocks, such as Gantt charts, timelines, or dashboards, to add advanced functionality to your base. Blocks provide insights and visualization capabilities.

7. Collaborate Effectively

- Share bases with teammates using specific permissions (editor, commenter, or read-only).
- Add comments to records for contextual collaboration.
- Use revision history to track changes and revert if needed.

8. Organize Your Workspace

- Group related bases within workspaces for better organization.
- Use consistent naming conventions for bases, tables, fields, and views to maintain clarity.

9. Keyboard Shortcuts for Speed

Memorize frequently used shortcuts to save time. For instance, navigating between views or quickly duplicating records can improve efficiency.

10. Regularly Back Up Your Data

Export your Airtable data periodically to ensure you have backups, especially for critical workflows.

Using keyboard shortcuts and implementing these productivity tips can transform how you work in Airtable. Whether you're managing complex projects or organizing personal tasks, these techniques will help you save time, stay organized, and achieve better results. Refer to this appendix whenever you need a quick boost in efficiency.

Appendix C: Additional Resources and Recommended Tools

As you continue your journey with Airtable, having access to the right resources and tools can significantly enhance your experience and productivity. This appendix lists additional resources to deepen your understanding of Airtable and recommended tools to complement and expand its functionality.

Airtable Official Resources

Airtable provides extensive resources to help users master the platform. Below are some essential links:

1. Airtable Help Center

- **URL**: https://support.airtable.com
- The Help Center is an extensive repository of articles and guides covering everything from basic setup to advanced features like automations and scripting.

2. Airtable Community Forum

- **URL**: https://community.airtable.com
- Join Airtable's community forum to interact with other users, share your workflows, and get answers to your questions.

3. Airtable Universe

- **URL**: https://www.airtable.com/universe
- Explore Airtable Universe for inspiration. It features real-world bases created by other users for various use cases, from content planning to personal budgeting.

4. Airtable Webinars and Tutorials

- **URL**: https://www.airtable.com/webinars
- Watch live and recorded webinars on specific topics, such as building workflows, using automations, and managing teams effectively.

5. Airtable YouTube Channel

- **URL**: https://www.youtube.com/c/Airtable
- Find video tutorials, success stories, and creative ways to use Airtable.

Recommended Tools and Extensions

1. Zapier

- **Website**: https://zapier.com
- **Purpose**: Automate workflows by connecting Airtable with thousands of other apps like Slack, Gmail, and Trello.
- **Key Features**:
    - Automate data entry from other tools into Airtable.
    - Trigger Airtable actions based on events in other apps.

2. Make (formerly Integromat)

- **Website**: https://www.make.com
- **Purpose**: Automate and integrate Airtable with advanced, customizable workflows.
- **Key Features**:
  - Complex multi-step automation.
  - Visual editor for creating integrations.

3. Softr

- **Website**: https://www.softr.io
- **Purpose**: Build no-code web apps and websites using Airtable as the backend.
- **Key Features**:
  - Create custom portals, directories, and dashboards.
  - Integrate Airtable data seamlessly into public-facing websites.

4. MiniExtensions

- **Website**: https://miniextensions.com
- **Purpose**: Add advanced features and functionalities to Airtable.
- **Key Features**:
  - Advanced forms with prefilled data.
  - Scheduled record updates and reminders.
  - File storage integration with Google Drive.

5. Pory

- **Website**: https://www.pory.io
- **Purpose**: Create member portals and web apps with Airtable data.
- **Key Features**:
  - Pre-built templates for specific use cases like CRMs and directories.
  - Drag-and-drop customization.

Learning Platforms

1. Udemy

- **URL**: https://www.udemy.com
- Find affordable Airtable courses, covering everything from beginner to advanced topics.

2. Skillshare

- **URL**: https://www.skillshare.com
- Offers classes on Airtable, productivity, and workflow optimization.

3. LinkedIn Learning

- **URL**: https://www.linkedin.com/learning
- Professional tutorials on Airtable and related tools for managing data and teams.

Analytics and Visualization Tools

1. Tableau

- **Website**: https://www.tableau.com
- **Purpose**: Visualize Airtable data with powerful analytics and dashboards.

2. Google Data Studio

- **Website**: https://datastudio.google.com
- **Purpose**: Create dynamic reports and dashboards by connecting Airtable data via third-party integrations.

Browser Extensions

1. Airtable Web Clipper

- **Purpose**: Save web content directly into your Airtable bases.
- **Availability**: Free from the Airtable website and browser extension stores.

2. Toggl Track

- **Website**: https://www.toggl.com/track
- **Purpose**: Track time spent on Airtable tasks and integrate results into your bases.

These resources and tools are designed to help you get the most out of Airtable. Whether you're automating workflows, building web apps, or analyzing data, the right tools and learning platforms can make your experience more seamless and powerful. Keep this appendix handy for quick access to resources that will help you maximize your productivity with Airtable.

Conclusion

Congratulations on completing **"Airtable Made Easy: From Data Management to Powerful Web Apps"**! By now, you've gained the knowledge and confidence to leverage Airtable for a variety of purposes, from managing data to creating powerful, no-code solutions. Whether you're building a simple task tracker or a dynamic web application, Airtable's versatility ensures that you have the tools to succeed.

Key Takeaways

Throughout this book, you've learned:

- The fundamentals of Airtable, including how it fits into the no-code movement.
- How to create and structure bases, customize field types, and organize your data effectively.
- The power of views, filters, and collaboration tools for team-based workflows.
- Advanced data linking techniques, including rollups, lookups, and master-detail relationships.
- How to design forms, automate workflows, and integrate with third-party services to streamline your processes.
- The potential of Airtable Interfaces to create custom applications and dashboards.
- Practical use cases across various industries to inspire your projects.
- Best practices to ensure your Airtable environment remains efficient, secure, and scalable as your needs grow.

The Path Ahead

Airtable is more than just a tool—it's a platform that evolves with you. As you continue to explore its capabilities, keep experimenting and innovating. Use Airtable's features to solve unique problems, simplify workflows, and build solutions tailored to your personal or professional needs.

Remember, the world of no-code is expanding rapidly, and Airtable is at the forefront of this movement. As Airtable introduces new features and integrations, revisit this book or explore the latest resources to keep up to date.

Stay Connected

The Airtable community is vibrant and supportive. Don't hesitate to:

- Join the **Airtable Community Forum** to share your experiences and learn from others.
- Explore **Airtable Universe** for templates and inspiration.
- Stay informed by following Airtable's updates and webinars.

A Final Word

Thank you for choosing this book as your guide. It has been a privilege to accompany you on this journey to mastering Airtable. As you move forward, let your creativity and problem-solving skills shine. With Airtable, the possibilities are endless.

Here's to your success with Airtable—may it transform the way you work and empower you to create incredible solutions!